Bedtime Stories for the Living
A Memoir

Jay Armstrong

The "Get Up" was first printed in Dear 2020: *Letters to a Year That Changed Everything* by Chris Palmore

First edition December 2021

Cover artwork by Amy R. Terlecki

Editing by Rachel Kobin

Book design by Melissa Desveaux

ISBN: (Print) 979-8-9852143-0-7

ISBN: (e-book) 979-8-9852143-1-4

Published by Write On Fight On LLC

https://jayarmstrongwrites.com

It's not important that you know everything about where I came from. About who I am. It's not important you know everything about my disease, about the specifics of the disease, or what it's like to have it. It's only important that you remember that behind every disease is a person. Remember that and you have everything you need to travel through my country.

—Simon Fitzmaurice, *It's Not Dark Yet*

I believe that what we become depends on what our fathers teach us at odd moments, when they aren't trying to teach us. We are formed by little scraps of wisdom.

—Umberto Eco, *Foucault's Pendulum*

For Haley, Chase, and Dylan

For Cindy, for always taking notes

ACKNOWLEDGMENTS

Writing a book, like living your life, seems to be a solo effort, but I've learned you can't do either alone. Many people, knowingly or unknowingly, helped me write this book. Cindy, Haley, Chase, and Dylan, thank you for your unwavering support, supplying me with material, and allowing me to write such a personal book. I'm sure living with a writer is not easy, and you provided me the space and time I needed to work. Also, thanks for not thinking I'm weird for spending so many hours squirreled away writing. To my parents, Greg and Donna, for your deep love, guidance, and kindness. For sitting with me and comforting me through so many doctor's appointments. For always caring. To my younger brothers Keith and Kyle and their wives, Danielle and Kait, for supporting me like I was your little brother. To my editor, Rachel Kobin and my copyeditor, Vee White, from Write Vision Services. This book would have not been possible without you two. You both encouraged me when I needed encouraging and you pushed me when I needed pushing. To my book designer Melissa Desveaux. I'm so lucky to have worked with you. Your guidance and patience alleviated much of my stress. To Steve Terlecki, for all your technical and creative help with Write On Fight On. To Amy R.Terlecki for designing the amazing cover for this book. Your vision and precision are true gifts. To the good men of Mancation—Casey, Jack, John, Marc, Mike, Pete, Rob, Steve, and Tim—for the twenty-five years of friendship, laughter, and Keystone. To all the students I have ever taught, but especially Wes Hart who convinced me I was a writer and who taught me the human story never graduates. To the astronauts/teachers I worked with on the Red Planet. You kept me in orbit. You kept me sane and laughing when sanity and laughter were like air on Mars. To all my doctors and physical therapists who helped me make sense of my illness. To "The Big Man" Andrew Patterson, Deb Bella, Aunt Glenda, Rich Teneyck, Fran McKenna, Gail Boenning, Mary Schantz, Blake Gilgore, Jesse Jackson, Clark Able, Deb Dauer (RIP), Aunt Susan (RIP), CB (RIP), the vigilantes of the "Write Club" and to everyone who has followed and supported Write On Fight On (writeonfighton.org) through the years. You inspired me when I needed inspiration. You allowed me to be vulnerable, to share my story, and reminded me life favors the brave. And last, I would like to thank the hole in my brain. You have gifted me with perseverance and patience. I am grateful for you. You changed not only my life but my perspective. Without you I would have never been able to write this book.

CONTENTS

INTRODUCTION   15

    BEFORE I TURN OUT THE LIGHTS: LETTER #1   21

PART I: WHEN LIFE HANDS YOU LEMONS   23

    THE PHONE CALL   24

    THE DAY I LEARNED I COULD NO LONGER JUMP   37

    SIGNS   46

    THE ADVENTURES OF CLARK ABLE AND ME   54

    HANDS   58

    THE "GET UP"   62

    MY UPCOMING PHOTO SHOOT (AND WHY YOU SHOULD TAKE A
WALK TODAY)   67

    DAD, IT'S YOUR TURN TO READ   72

    SPEECH THERAPY   78

    THE MOMENT IN WHICH EVERYTHING IS DIFFERENT   83

    DON'T GIVE UP   88

    BEFORE I TURN OUT THE LIGHTS: LETTER #2   92

PART II: YOU'RE ONLY YOUNG ONCE   97

    "DAD, WHY IS IT RAINING?"   98

    LEARNING TO BREATHE TOGETHER   101

    HALEY BECOMES A WRITER   104

    FATHER-DAUGHTER QUARANTINE PROJECT   107

    A LITTLE MORAL COURAGE   116

SEX EDUCATION WITH THE ARMSTRONGS   119

DYLAN LEARNS TO RIDE A BIKE   125

CHASE LEARNS THE "F-WORD"   127

PARENTS OF THE YEAR   132

BEFORE I TURN OUT THE LIGHTS: LETTER # 3   140

PART III: YOU'LL UNDERSTAND WHEN YOU'RE OLDER   149

HOW TO CROSS A THRESHOLD   150

THE WINK   154

THE GOOD CANCER   164

THE WORKING MAN RETIRES   168

THE PLAN   173

WHY YOU SHOULD READ THE ALCHEMIST WHEN YOU'RE OLDER   176

A GOOD MOMENT (IN A YEAR OF BAD MOMENTS)   182

PRIDE BEFORE THE FALL   186

THE FIRST DAY OF THE REST OF MY LIFE   192

A PEACEFUL TRANSFER OF POWER   204

GETTING BOOED   209

THE "GET UP": THE REMIX   213

BEFORE I TURN OFF THE LIGHTS: LETTER #4   217

PART IV: I'M NOT SLEEPING; I'M JUST RESTING MY EYES   223

GOOD ADVICE NEVER DIES   224

BOWLING WITH GOD   228

ADVICE FROM THE DEAD   234

MY WORST DAY AS A TEACHER   240

CELEBRATING VICTORY WITH THE DEAD   244

WRITING TO RAISE THE DEAD   249

OLD MAN AND THE TEE   254

BEFORE I TURN OUT THE LIGHTS: LETTER #5   258

PART V: A MAN CANNOT BE A FATHER WITHOUT LOVE   263

FIFTEEN YEARS OF IMPROV (AND MARRIAGE)   264

HOW TO SAVE A MARRIAGE   269

THE LOVE STORY THAT ALMOST NEVER HAPPENED   273

TAKING NOTES: A LOVE STORY   277

BEFORE I TURN OUT THE LIGHTS: LETTER #6   282

BEDTIME STORY PROMPTS   285

BIBLIOGRAPHY   287

Photograph courtesy of Jackie Murphy Photography, LLC. 2020.

INTRODUCTION

There is something you should know. In the history of my ordinary suburban life, I've never told any of my three children a bedtime story. Not telling your child a bedtime story seems like a major dad offense. Like forgetting them at Target or wearing a clown costume to "Back-to-School Night" or letting them swim twenty-six minutes after lunch.

Do I love my children?

On most days I do.

On most days, like you, they're decent people. So why didn't I tell them bedtime stories?

Selfishly, I don't like the pressure. The nightlight. The slow swirl of the ceiling fan blades. Their big eyes staring up at me, expecting me to entertain them, to stir their imagination. Who do they think I am? Bruce Springsteen? No. I'm a dad who gets his sushi from a supermarket. I wear sneakers with khaki pants. I once taught high school English in New Jersey. I mean, to be creative and tell a story on demand is down-right stressful. Who needs that kind of stress after 9 p.m.?

My parents were better parents. When I was a kid, Mom and Dad would tuck me into bed and tell me stories about my grandfathers and grandmothers, about how Mom and Dad met, or about playing stickball in narrow Philadelphia streets. Bedtime stories were history. They brought my little universe into focus, shaped my identity, and instilled a love of storytelling.

As good suburban boys do, I fell in love, got married, and had three kids. Just when things were going as planned, in 2013, I was diagnosed with a progressive brain disease called diffuse *cerebellar atrophy*. The disease degenerates my motor skills, balance, coordination, eyesight, and speech. A fall can lead to a head injury and weakening esophageal muscles to choking and asphyxiation, and so on—a veritable smorgasbord of potentially fatal complications. Two years later, sarcoidosis, a complicated autoimmune disorder that attacks every major body organ, was added to my list of health issues.

It was only when the prospect of death became real that I began writing.

In 2015, I created Write On Fight On (writeonfighton.org), and for the next five years I wrote and posted bedtime stories I never told my kids. By writing these stories, I began to reexamine who I once was, who I am now, and the man and father I hoped to one day grow up to be. Writing made me realize, in the face of our inevitable death, our time to tell our story is painfully brief. And that we should make like Springsteen and do what we can to achieve our dreams.

As I wrote this book, time passed. The kids grew up. My diseases progressed. People I love died. And one spring morning, standing in the driveway with my hands in my pockets, time's yellow chariot turned the corner. The air brakes exhaled, "Bye Dad" was said, and as the bus, my children, and a swirl of exhaust smoke disappeared down the street, I realized the irony of my effort. I was trying to preserve time while it was passing like a school bus in the morning. We can't stop time. We can only slow time by doing what we love. Doing the things that make us feel alive. And I have never been more alive than when telling a story.

This is a book of bedtime stories for the living. Stories that, if I did my job well, slow time, and make you and me glad to be alive. These stories are real. Or as real as memory allows them to be. As I discovered, life is both a funny and a heartbreaking experience. These stories are the moments I want to share with you because I believe, deep in my dad heart, we all have stories worth sharing.

I came across an article about how, in the mid-1990s, Dr. Marshall Duke and Dr. Robyn Fivush of Emory University developed and conducted a twenty-question survey of children entitled, "Do You Know" which asked them about their families. The results showed that the more stories, both positive and negative, the children knew about their family's history, the more resilient the children tended to be. As the study concluded, knowing family stories was "the single best predictor of children's emotional health and happiness." For better or worse, our family stories help us navigate our own troubles. Stories gift us courage when we're afraid, offer direction when we're lost, or comfort when we're lonely.

Dear reader, please know that I'm humbled you are reading this book. Thank you. I hope my stories help you, give you permission to dream, and maybe give you the strength to tell your own stories. I hope you paid full price for this book because college for three ain't free.

But if this book doesn't offer my children financial prosperity, more than anything, this book is a gift for them. It's a family history, an instruction manual, an honest reflection about a fleeting moment, a smile, a glance, and the goodnight kiss I often failed to give them.

Maybe one day, when they're lost or confused or angry or sad or daydreaming about the prom queen, they will open this book and read a story or one of the letters I've written to them. Maybe my words will let them hear my voice again. Feel my lips pressed against their ears. And maybe they'll know they're not alone. That Dad is here. With them. Helping them through life forever.

Be well,

Jay

Hemingway smelled oranges for inspiration. I smell the baseball I caught at the MLB Homerun Derby in Philadelphia in 1996.

BEFORE I TURN OUT THE LIGHTS: LETTER #1

Dear Haley, Chase, and Dylan,

As I was writing this book, one of you started a nightly ritual before you scampered off to bed. You'd say, "Good night. I love you. See you in the morning." The habit caught on and became a family mantra. When you said this, my head was often buried in the computer, swirling with doubt and writer's block. I paused long enough to give the halfhearted, rushed reply of, "Goodnight.Iloveyou.Seeyouinthemorning."

Shamefully, I often failed to be present when you yearned for my attention one final time that day. I should have put down my work. I should have looked you in the eyes. I should have given those sentences the annunciation they deserved.

Life whistles by. You will learn, maybe when you become parents, that moments—especially with your children—are often hastily lived. Like me, you might let your work consume you and grow less attuned to life. Your head might become a drum of meetings and presentations and conference calls. These mundane noises assume precedence over the more important, sublime sounds like the patter of approaching feet before sunrise or the squeal of laughter at dinner that echoes in your memory. Whatever you grow up to become—a writer or a baseball player or simply a suburban parent—heed your father's advice. Don't close your ears. Listen to what life is saying.

Good night.

I love you.

See you in the morning.

PART I: WHEN LIFE HANDS YOU LEMONS

THE PHONE CALL

It's twenty minutes until varsity soccer practice begins. I'm in my classroom watching Danny write a potential roster for the upcoming season on the white board.

"Coach, do you really want to put four freshmen on varsity?"

"No. I don't." I check the clock. "But do we have a choice?"

Danny and I look over the list of names in silence.

"Coach?"

"Yeah Danny."

"This is going to be a rough season."

I look at him and smile. "I might be doing a lot of drinking this year."

"Cool. I'm down with getting drunk."

Danny is twenty-two, one of my former players, and now my unpaid assistant coach. During his four years as a student, I'd never taught Danny, mainly because I taught Advanced Placement English classes. Danny would frequent my class, however, knowing that since the smart kids liked to read and talked quietly about what he called "English stuff," the corners of my classroom made perfect crannies for him to curl up in and take a midday nap. Danny has since graduated. He's a host at TGI Friday's and the self-proclaimed "Dopest Host on the East Coast." He's a bit doughier than he was four years ago. He's a good kid, dependable and always happy. But Danny is locked in that awkward stage of development, acting like an eighteen-year-old while trying to present himself as an adult. I'm thirty-four and have the same problem. Maybe that's why we get along so well. As Danny continues to write and erase names on the white board, my cell phone rings. It's my general practitioner Dr. Thomas. The sight of his phone number makes my skin jump and my stomach bottom out in fear. Call it intuition or being in tune with the universe, but I knew bad news lurked on the other line. It's funny how that works. How a "bad news phone call" seems to have a slightly distorted ring that gives you an electric, sinking sensation.

"Hello?"

"Jason, this is Dr. Thomas."

"Hey. How are you?"

"We got your test results back." His voice is flat and his use of declarative sentences scares me.

"Jason, your blood tests came back fine. However, your MRI reveals something significant. Do you have a minute?"

"Significant?" Hearing the word *significant* made me think oh, "significant." *That's a good thing. It's like saying, "My significant other makes the best burritos," or "Sorry the bed is so lumpy, I stuffed a significant amount of money under the mattress.*

"Jason, your images show significant *cerebellar atrophy*. Are you familiar with the term *cerebellar atrophy*?"

I thought, then spoke. "I know the cerebellum is part of the brain. I know atrophy means to shrink. Are you saying my cerebellum has shrunk, doctor?"

"Yes. Your images reveal significant thinning of your cerebellum, which occurs when brain cells die." I somehow forgot *significant* can also have negative connotations.

"Die?"

Danny stares at me, pointing to the list of names on the board. He proudly mouths, "I got it!"

Dr. Thomas continues, "Jason, this is serious. Since this is the baseline image, we don't know the rate at which the atrophy is occurring. The cerebellum controls muscle movement, balance, coordination, and eye movement. If you're having complications in those areas, suffice to say your cerebellum has atrophied significantly."

For a moment, neither of us says anything. His silence makes me believe he's delivered bad news over the phone before. There's grace in his silence. He's giving me a few breaths to digest the immediate facts of my life.

"Jason, I went ahead and scheduled an appointment for you with Dr. Paul Simon tomorrow at 10 a.m. He's a local neurologist and a friend of mine who can answer your questions better than I can. I urge you to rearrange your plans to make that appointment."

"Okay."

After giving me Dr. Simon's address, he says a few other things but all I hear is, "Good luck and God bless."

Dr. Thomas had hung up. With the phone still against my ear, I look over at Danny. He's laughing. He just wrote the word "poop" on the board. Danny loves the word poop. I've found poop printed on Post-it notes on my desk and on my game-day lineup. Or etched into the Styrofoam of my Dunkin Donuts coffee cup. When Danny feels extra creative, he follows the word with a steaming illustration.

I want to call my wife.

I pull the phone from my ear, punch up Cindy's phone number, and stare at her name. I picture her at home in the backyard watching the kids splash around in the kiddie pool. She's wearing sunglasses and is stretched across a blue blanket with a glass of iced tea alongside her smooth brown thighs. She's smiling with our young children, and they're happy. Life, as they know it, is perfect.

I look at Danny, force a smile, and hang up the phone before Cindy can answer.

"Let's go to practice, Danny."

"Hey, Coach, check out the board."

"Poop is right Danny." Poop is right.

Practice ends, and I sit in my car. The keys are in my lap. I had hesitated to call Cindy. To shift the car into drive toward home. Toward uncertainty. Life was going to be different now. I held a secret that was going to turn our life on its head. My tongue pressed hard against the diagnosis. It was powerful. Terrifying. And the longer I kept the secret, the longer life continued as planned.

But before I could leave the parking lot, I shared my secret with Cindy. I repeat the conversation I had with Dr. Thomas. Her voice quivers as she asks me to spell *cerebellar atrophy*. I know she is taking notes. Dylan cries. He is six weeks old. I tell Cindy I'll be home soon and hang up. I know she is crying now. I do the same. Not a sobbing oh-Nicholas-Sparks-stop-pulling-at-my-heartstrings cry. Just hard, chest chokes. Like the car is suddenly short on air.

I am scared.

I get home. Since we're twenty-first century beings—who, when we don't understand something like how to grout tile or make banana bread, we Google it—Cindy and I retreat to the computer and look up *cerebellar atrophy*.

There is nothing like that first Google search for your degenerative brain condition. The eighteen seconds it takes the internet to produce 1.2 million results is agonizing. Amazingly, it only takes about five seconds of scanning the results to scare the ~~poop~~ shit out of me. When I read the words *irreversible*, and *paralysis*, and *death* out loud, Cindy grips my hand and says, "Let's see the doctor before you start diagnosing yourself."

I close the laptop and hugged her, and we cried together. Nicholas Sparks style.

Later that night, after the kids are asleep, Cindy and I have one of those adult conversations regarding the news of the day. We decide she'll take the kids to school the next morning and go to work and that my mom will accompany me to the appointment with Dr. Simon.

It's amazing how the spectrum of your life can change so drastically in a matter of hours. One minute you're watching Danny laugh at *poop* and next you are on the couch with your wife, tracing her nervous knuckles with your thumb, talking quietly about your degenerative brain condition. And that's the thing. If the news of the day had been Danny's poop fixation, Cindy would have listened. We've been together since we were sixteen. In that time she has listened to me tell hundreds of stories—some funny, some sad. Trite stories about work. Booze-fueled degenerate stories that only the four people involved find funny. Stories that aren't really stories, more like Seinfeldian musings on life. But she listened. Always.

30

Cindy had taught me the power of listening. How the deliberate act of listening has nothing to do with the topic and everything to do with honoring the relationship. Look, I'm no Dr. Phil, but I've come to believe that listening, truly listening to someone, is the greatest compliment you can give them. It's like saying, "Hey, we're both tragic creatures, but for this nugget of time I'm going to put away my tragedy to focus on yours."

I believe we all want to be heard. And if you can find spouses, friends, colleagues, and doctors who will listen to you, I implore you to hold them close because sooner or later we all need someone to talk to.

Dr. Paul Simon's office was tucked in a nondescript office complex I had spent most of my life driving by. Mom and I enter the office and step into 1976: cherry wood paneled walls and an orangey matted carpet. Framed pictures of waterfalls and hand painted horses tacked randomly in the waiting room. A receptionist sits with the back of her head to us in what looks like a penalty box. She looks like a receptionist plucked from a 70s high school yearbook. High gray hair, purple turtleneck, big and tinted reading glasses. She clangs away on a typewriter even though there's a perfectly good computer on her desk. It wouldn't have surprised me if Doc Brown and Marty McFly were in the waiting room discussing Flux Capacitors. Beyond the penalty box is another little room stacked floor to ceiling with manila file folders.

Old-school files before hard drives and flash drives and computers.

The receptionist takes my name and my fifteen-dollar co-pay and tells us to have a seat. The waiting room is empty and seems like it may have been empty for a long time. The pleather chairs look like yard sale leftovers and the coffee table could have been the one your grandmother had in her living room. *Good Day Philadelphia* airs on a tube TV. A segment on fall fashion trends for men informs me that red capris are in and khaki-colored khakis are so last year, which make sense since I'm wearing khaki-colored khakis. Everything in the office, even my pants, are from another time.

Mom sits with the back of her head pressed against the panel wall. Her eyes are closed. She looks tired and I have a feeling these last few hours have been tougher on her than on me.

A nurse enters the waiting room and calls my name. She wears pink modern scrubs, and a rose tattoo is inked on her right forearm. She looks out of place. Like she had wandered into Mike Brady's living room. She smiles and tells us to follow her, and I feel a little more at ease. She leads us down a hallway into the biggest examination room I've ever been in. Aside from the obligatory examination table, there are two chairs, another coffee table, a changing closet, and a fish tank with a Fat Nemo clownfish floating inside. There is a hi-fi record player with wooden speakers that share a shelf with gift shop knickknacks: a mug announcing, "Virginia is for Lovers," a miniature Statue of Liberty, a snow globe with the Golden Gate Bridge inside, and a glass ashtray from St. Louis. And in a way, the weird, the tacky Americana decor magnifies the absurdity of the last twenty-four hours of my life.

Dr. Paul Simon hurries into the room studying the printouts of my MRI. He stops and stands in the middle of the room with his eyes glued to the MRI as Mom, Fat Nemo, and I wait. When he looks up, Dr. Simon bears an uncanny resemblance to his famous namesake in a lab coat. Of course, he is not the *that* Paul Simon. But in moments of crushing heartbreak, everything feels distorted. It's difficult to tell where fantasies end and reality begins.

"Jason Armstrong?"

"Hello."

"Can I call you Jay?"

"'You Can Call Me Al.'"

Dr. Simon didn't laugh.

If you didn't laugh, I suggest you familiarize yourself with Paul Simon songs right now. I'll wait. I always play music for my children. My father played music for me. In troubled times, I've found great refuge in the comfort of song. As I tell you the rest of this story, I'll make allusions to Paul Simon songs. My hope is that when you finish reading, you'll retreat to your music and discover comfort in some Paul Simon songs too. My personal favorites are woven into the rest of this story. See if you can find them.

He continues to study the MRI. Except for the bubbles from Fat Nemo's fish tank, there is only "The Sound of Silence." Finally, he says, "Jason, when did these symptoms start?"

I tell him about my dizziness and leg weakness that began a few weeks ago. He listens, standing with his arms folded, occasionally scribbling on a yellow notepad. His demeanor is professional and reserved until I tell him that after I spoke to Dr. Thomas yesterday, I'd been doing some research on my own.

He looks up. "So, you're playing doctor?"

I sense I'm standing on a "Bridge Over Troubled Water."

"No. Just curious."

"Okay, so what do you think you have?

"Excuse me?"

"From your Googling, what do you think you have? I'll tell

you if you have it or not."

I'm suddenly thrown into a game of diagnosis roulette. I look at Mom. I look at Fat Nemo.

"ALS?"

"No."

"Huntington's Disease?"

"No."

"Cancer?"

"No."

"Doctor, this is not a fun game."

"I understand. Do you want to know what I think you have?"

Sheepishly, I answer, "Yes."

He explains my MRI clearly reveals a diffuse *cerebellar atrophy.* However, it is his opinion the atrophy can indicate the onset of Parkinson's or a form of spinocerebellar ataxia, or SCA for short.

Thanks to Marty McFly, I knew about Parkinson's. SCA sounded scary, and I didn't ask. But Mom did. Moms are good for that.

Asking the hard questions their children would rather avoid.

"There are many different strands of SCA. And we can't know which strand Jason has until he has more testing. Some strands progress slowly over years and others progress quickly and are fatal."

I looked at Mom. Then at Fat Nemo. Neither say a word.

Dr. Simon writes a few scripts for me and urges me to get tests and blood work done immediately. He also says he wants me to go see Dr. Reardon, a renowned neurologist at Jefferson Hospital in Philadelphia.

Mom and I leave the office in silence and as we cross the parking lot she slips her arm through mine and rests her head on my shoulder. If I was a dead man walking, Mom just wants to be as close to me as life allows. Mom had always been that way. Trying to take away her son's pain. So much of what I have written in this book is my attempt to feel what Mom has felt. To recognize the deep, uncompromising love that welds the bond between parent and child. "A Mother and Child Reunion."

We get into the car and Mom drives toward the testing center while I Google spinocerebellar ataxia on my phone.

"Homeward Bound." I wish I were.

THE DAY I LEARNED I COULD NO LONGER JUMP

Chase is in the backyard, dribbling the length of the patio and shooting at a little net he received for his fourth birthday. He's six now and he's getting good at basketball: dribbling, jump shots, and layups. He's quickly discovering the earthly battle between the human body and gravity.

Chase makes a jump shot and celebrates. As it often happens with sons, he can feel the weight of his father's eyes on him. He looks up with his blue eyes to see me framed in the window.

"Come out and play, Dad!"

I smile and wave as a trapdoor in my stomach drops open and my heart falls through and keeps falling because I can't play. Not now. Not today. Because some days my body aches too much. Because some days my brain does weird things. Some days my brain convinces me I'm trapped on a Tilt-a-Whirl or I'm buckled to the back of a gigantic black bird or I'm a sneaker in the dryer or a frat-party drunkard. Because some days the world spins, glides, tumbles, and wobbles off its axis at speeds beyond what my eyes and the undamaged parts of my brain can comprehend.

And, some days, I don't play because I simply can't risk the embarrassment.

To be honest, I've avoided writing this story for some time now. I guess by writing it, by pinning down its facts, I'm forced to accept certain truths. I assume I did what most of us do when we don't have the energy, courage, or conviction to deal with truth. We tuck it away, in the darkness of a desk drawer, like a debt, and do our best to forget about it.

But memories, with just the right stimulus, can resurrect without benediction. They sit up, blink, open the drawer and leap into the light to remind you that memories, like debts, can be avoided for only so long before they must be attended to.

The stimulus today is a basketball bouncing off the concrete.

In January 2014 it was six months after I'd been diagnosed with cerebellar degeneration. It was six months after a neurologist examined an MRI of my brain, leveled his eyes, cleared his throat, and said, "You should be dead or in a hospital bed." I was staring at my physical therapist, Denise, and she was daring me to jump.

"Jay, I want you to jump."

"Like up and down?"

"Yes, like jump up and down."

I smiled and looked around the St. Lawrence Rehabilitation Center. There are three other patients in the activity center with me. Two women, both walking on a treadmill, and Bill, a former Navy captain who was the proud owner of a new titanium hip. Bill was pedaling a stationary bike and, according to St. Lawrence lore, Bill had never smiled. Ever.

I was the youngest one in the activity center by at least twenty years. This was problematic because comparison feeds fiction. Surveying the room, like the true gym class hero I still thought I was, I swelled with pride believing I was the most enabled in the room.

I said, "Denise, need I remind you that I'm an athlete. A collegiate soccer player. I've been jumping my whole life."

Denise playfully rolled her eyes.

This was only my third appointment, but Denise and I

already shared chemistry. It was January. Playoff football. I'm an Eagles fan. She's a Giants fan. Between sets of squats and leg raises I told her Eli Manning is overrated. She told me the stereotypes about the jerkiness of Eagles fans are apparently true.

Denise dressed primly—a turtleneck, no earrings, no rings, just a silver cross pinned to her sweatshirt. But she was funny and real, and in just our few hours together, I realized she was the most compassionate person I had ever met.

During a set of lunges, Denise told me Bill had just lost his wife of forty years to breast cancer. Then her brown eyes welled up with tears and she said she had lost her grandmother to the same disease. Denise and I both looked at Bill. We watched him slowly pedal. She told me it was her goal to make him smile today.

For this story, I need you to suspend reality. I need you to believe the unbelievable, but the unbelievable is the truth. Truth that the National Institutes of Health in Bethesda, Maryland, the epicenter of rare and novel diseases, couldn't believe.

Before my diagnosis, I believed that I would do physically heroic dad things like carry all three children off to bed like footballs, each tucked under my arm, after they had fallen asleep on the couch. I believed I would be the MVP of father-son baseball games. I believed my children and I would run 5k's together, and I believed on a perfect summer morning, when the sky was veined with golden light, we would ride bikes along the New Jersey coastline.

But we age and learn that real life always falls incredibly short of the one we imagined, of the one we planned. And yet, despite our protests, it's the unplanned life that teaches us more than our fantasies ever could.

"Jay, are you ready?" Denise said.

"Eagles are always ready to fly."

"Ok, but I'll be right here, beside you, just in case."

Bill continued to ride the stationary bike. He was straight-faced and staring at me.

"Hey Denise, can you go make Bill smile? He's freaking me out."

"Just concentrate on what you're doing."

"Denise, I got this. Need I remind you again: I'm an athlete."

Cerebellar degeneration is exactly as it sounds. There is massive cell loss in the cerebellum, known as the little brain. The little brain controls motor skills: coordination, vision, and balance. After examinations by some of the top neurologists in the country, no one

knew if I was born with a gaping hole in my cerebellum and had been

able to compensate my whole life until now, or if a civil war had

erupted in my little brain where cells attacked and killed each other.

As I write this, as Chase drills a jump shot, no one knows if the war is

over.

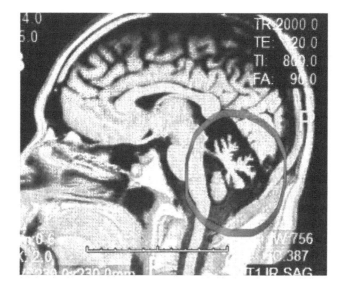

*Inside the circle is what's left of my cerebellum. This area should be
full of brain.*

Given the size of the hole in my brain, doctors are surprised

by how well I look, speak, and function. For a brief period, my doctors

thought I had ALS. Then they thought Huntington's disease. Then MS.

Then, after six months of testing, they simply shrugged their collective shoulders and said they didn't know. They told me, as if they were riding the Tilt-a-Whirl or the giant bird with me, to "just hold on." I had been holding on, but over the last few months, my coordination, vision, balance and motor skills had all deteriorated. Not at breakneck speed, but slowly, methodically. Little things, things I've taken for granted—handwriting, climbing stairs, and carrying a few bags of groceries—have become difficult.

Denise leveled her eyes into mine.

"I want you to jump."

"How high?"

"As high as you can."

I bent my knees, swung my arms back and forth, and tried to jump. I tried and tried and tried and tried, but I just couldn't do it. I just couldn't force my feet to leave the floor. My big brain screamed at my little brain, "Jump!" But the message was not delivered. It were as if some internal chord that transmitted important messages had been severed.

To Denise, Bill, and the two ladies on the treadmill, I must have looked ridiculous, like a wide-eyed field mouse fixed in a glue trap.

I shook my head. "Jump!" "Jump!"

"It's okay, Jay. You don't have to do it."

"No, Denise. I can jump. I have to jump."

"Relax. Take a seat. Let me check on Bill."

Denise returned, told me she offered Bill her best joke about a priest, a rabbi, and a monk playing Monopoly in Mexico but he didn't crack. Didn't even flinch

"Denise, I've had enough for today."

When you think of your future self, you envision your best self. Happy and unblemished. You're the hero of your own movie. You convince yourself that you, unlike everyone else, won't end up a tragedy. In those great moments of fantasy you believe, with a swollen heart, in your own fiction.

I limped into the locker room, found a folding chair, stared into my lap, and began to digest the fact that I had lost the ability to jump. It occurred to me, right there in that empty locker room on that folding chair, that I would not be the man, the father, I had envisioned. A father running, jumping through life, with his children. A father playing basketball in the backyard with his son. A father who is fast and coordinated and who teaches his boy the aerodynamics of a layup as the evening sun vanishes from the suburban sky.

I opened the locker room door to find Bill in the hallway, sitting in his wheelchair, as if he were waiting for me.

I offered a little half-smile and before I could turn, Bill spoke, "Hey." He still had those steely gray Navy captain eyes, eyes that didn't look at you, eyes that looked through you. Bill cleared his throat, shifted his weight on his God-given hip, and said, "Don't give up, kid."

"Thanks."

And then, in a subtle, unprompted way, Bill smiled.

SIGNS

Cindy pokes her head into the living room. "Do you want to go on a quick Target trip with me?"

Feet up, relaxing in the recliner, I'm reading Tommy Orange's heartbreaking novel *There, There* about twelve Native Americans struggling to accept their complex and painful history. I glance over at Clark Able in the corner of the room. Clark is leaning against the wall. Like he's waiting for a bus or a store manager. He's been quiet for weeks, just leaning over and waiting. Patiently. Every time I pass Clark Able, I think, *Is this the day*? But it hasn't been. Until today.

A few weeks ago, I ordered Clark Able off Amazon. He cost me nineteen dollars and ninety-nine cents. Clark Able is an adjustable, collapsible, free-standing, walking cane made of fine American metal and plastic that earned four and a half out of five stars.

Ken from the United States said, "It's well made and easy to walk with."

Aisha from Canada said, "All in all it was a good buy."

Kathryn from the United States bought it for her trip to Ireland. You know, with the hills and cobblestones, and she was "thrilled with the purchase."

A week before Clark Able was wrapped in packing bubbles, folded in a brown box, and dropped on my front step, I endured an embarrassing walk on the beach. I stumbled and staggered like my legs had no joints. Like I was drunk. But I wasn't drunk. It was just my ataxia, one of the symptoms of cerebellar degeneration, which makes it hard for me to coordinate my muscles. Ataxia and uneven surfaces do not mix well.

I named my walking cane Clark Able because of the obvious play on Clark Gable, "The King of Hollywood." But also after the hardworking writer Clark Kent—Superman's Earthly alias. And then there's William Clark, half of the famed Lewis and Clark duo, who courageously traversed from the Mississippi River to California in 1804. And finally, Clark W. Griswold—the lovable, slightly neurotic suburban father who, whether it was driving his family from Chicago to California or hosting a Christmas vacation, just wanted the best for his family. Clark is resilient like a punching bag is resilient. I see a lot of myself in all of those Clarks. Also, Clark Able's initials are CA. Which are the initials of *cerebellar atrophy.*

From my recliner, I evaluate the situation: *It's Wednesday, July 15th at 10 a.m. Target probably won't be crowded. I probably won't see anyone I know.* I look at Clark Able in the corner. Waiting. Like Superman, puffing out his chest, waiting for duty to call.

"Sure, I'll go," I finally answer Cindy's question.

"I'm leaving in twenty minutes," she says.

Do you ever feel like the universe is trying to tell you something? Like if you looked close enough or listened long enough, you would see a sign or hear a message that was meant only for you? Have you ever told someone about your signs only to have them shake their head and look at you incredulously?

This is a story about signs.

I close the book, "unrecline," wobble across the living room and up the stairs, and open the second drawer in the dresser. I find my gray "Life favors the brave. #writeonfighton" T-shirt folded on top, waiting for me. A sign.

When I come back downstairs, I move toward the living

room corner and grab Clark Able. "Are you bringing that?" Cindy asks.

There are moments in your life when you second guess yourself. When you mull over the familiar question, "Is this a good idea?" Buying a house, going to grad school, reaching for a second cheeseburger. I consider the *that* at the end of Cindy's question. *That* seems louder than all of the other words. What will *that* make me look like to others? Disabled? Helpless? A victim? A fake? We make or fail to make so many decisions for fear of how they might look to other people. I'm guilty of hiding my disease from others. I'm so afraid to look weak or broken that I would rather live a lie. I take a deep breath. *Relax.*

"Yes."

"Cool."

And that was that.

Cindy, Clark Able, and I arrive at Target. The parking lot is scattered with cars. As we walk through the parking lot, Clark makes a click-click-click sound. I like it. A rhythm to my walk. And when I walk with him, it's like walking with the cool kid, "The King of Hollywood," I feel—cool.

The three of us enter Target through electric doors and into the air-conditioning. We first turn right, but there are printed signs that warn, "Wrong Way." Literal signs.

Cindy, Clark, and I stop and look at each other.

People wearing masks stare at us as they stand, six feet apart, in the checkout line. It feels like a strange dream. The signs, the masks, the social distancing, the shiny white tile floor, the fluorescent lights, and the fear that aches in all of those eyes. One woman wearing a pink mask leans against a mini-refrigerator stocked with different colors of soda and tells another woman she's waiting to speak to the manager. This is not a dream. This is 2020. This is America. This is Target.

The three of us make a U-turn and head the other way. At the end of the aisle, coming toward us, is an old man walking like old men do on wobbly knees. He's wearing what my grandfather wears in every memory I have of him—a long-sleeve flannel shirt tucked into his blue jeans. A thick brown belt.

He's wearing a plain-white mask, a sign of present times.

But unlike my grandfather, who almost never wears hats in my memories—he's wearing a blue cap stitched with a battleship on it that hides, what appears to be, a full head of silver hair. He has blue eyes and thick hands like my grandfather did, and he's walking with a walking stick just like my grandfather so often did.

My grandfather's walking sticks hang in my house.

Cindy walks in front of me and talks about what we need to get. Something about a Chromebook. Something about one of our kids. Something about school in September.

Signs are personal. Like the universe is whispering to you, and only to you, a secret. If you choose to listen, the world fades and gets quiet and all you can hear is the secret.

Like with Bill from the St. Lawrence Rehabilitation Center, the old man and I meet eyes. Our eyes meet our canes. He still has wide shoulders and a thick chest. Maybe he was an athlete once. He nods at me. As if inviting me into a secret society, an ancient order: "Men with Canes."

I nod back.

The universe approves.

A sign.

When the three of us get back into the car, Cindy cranks the ignition. The radio DJ transitions from DJ talk to a song: "Broken" by lovelytheband. I listen. The music kicks in. The singer croons he likes broken people, because broken people remind him of his own brokenness.

Clark Able sits beside me. My brain spins. *Of all the songs, of all the refrains that could be played at this exact moment in time on this exact radio station—"*

A sign.

If we're willing to pay attention, I believe the universe, in its own unique language, speaks to us in subtle ways.

I believe in signs.

How could I not? A trinity of signs. As if the DJ, the old man with the Navy hat who looked like my grandfather, and my gray "Life favors the brave" shirt had called a meeting and hashed out a plan to nudge me when I needed nudging.

As if the universe was whispering secret advice to me. As if the universe knew this quick trip to Target on a Wednesday morning was a good time to offer my uncertain soul the certainty of signs.

THE ADVENTURES OF CLARK ABLE AND ME

I'm standing on the beach, a few feet from the waterline with the sun setting behind me. The pink and gold sky tumbles with tufts of cotton candy clouds before me. Looking around, I notice my fellow beach goers are not looking at me. A young couple snuggles on a red blanket, a man in a white hat sits by himself in the lifeguard stand smoking a cigar, and a woman walks a big dog who wags his tail and chews on a blue rubber ball. Snuggles, Stogie Joe, and Chewy don't notice the significance of Clark Able and me standing at the ocean's edge, with the beach behind us, like a pair of conquering kings.

When Holden Caulfield invites a sex worker to his hotel room in Chapter 13 of *The Catcher in the Rye*, he introduces himself as Jim Steele. You don't have to be a literary scholar to see what is going on there: Holden, an insecure, whiny, seventeen-year-old boy uses a pseudonym to present himself as a confident, secure man who has done this kind of thing before. In this moment, with Clark by my side, I breathe in the salty air, puff out my chest, and pretend to feel what Jim Steele must feel even when he's sleeping.

I told you I bought Clark after an ataxia-influenced wobbly walk on the beach. Walking on the sand, like drinking tequila, does something evil to my brain. For the most part, my cerebellum behaves like a schoolboy when I walk on flat surfaces. But on sand my cerebellum shucks and jives like a frat boy on spring break. I spent a good part of the summer worrying what people would think when they saw me with Clark Able. But isn't this how life works? We spend our precious time worrying about things beyond our control? It's why we don't get that haircut, or wear those shoes, or get that neck tattoo of a dragon with a rose dangling from its teeth, or walk with Clark Able.

I look around and nobody is looking at me. And frankly—no one cares. The couple, the dog, the man, are busy with their own lives.

"Can you take a picture of me?"

"Right now?" asks Cindy.

"Not now. I'm sitting like an old man in a beach chair. Let me get up."

With Clark Able's help, I pull myself and wobble a few feet

forward. I tell Cindy to take a few pictures of me and Clark Able. Here's the best one. Maybe you can tell, by my raised and glowing ear lobes, I'm smiling.

Clark Able and I taking in the view.

We're all self-absorbed with our own troubles. Like a stage actor who forgot their lines, we think ourselves into paralysis. We feel like the world is watching us. The truth is—it's not. In fact, the world is fat with things that are way more interesting than our skinny lives. Like clouds puffed out like cotton candy.

The modern person desperately struggles with self-acceptance, which comes from recognizing that we are enough. But this recognition is so difficult. It's why Holden Caulfield introduced himself as Jim Steele. *If I do this, what will they say about me?*

We are the stories we tell ourselves, and our stories persuade our behavior. When we narrate our own story, as opposed to letting others narrate for us, we become more self-assured and are more likely to make decisions that align with the personal narrative we desire. When we allow the critic, the person controlling the "like" button to control us, we will remain unhappy. Modern life conditions us to always look outside for validation. Instagram. Facebook. Tik-Tok. Our posts are scored by likes and shares. We've allowed our self-worth to be a product of other's opinions.

I turn from the ocean back to the beach. The sun winks behind the Ferris wheel spokes as Cindy watches our children play baseball in the cool sand. The couple, Stogie Joe, and the dog all have their lips on something. Their minds on something. Their hearts on something.

And that something isn't me.

HANDS

For the first few years of my elementary school experience,
Sister Thomas came to the classroom and led the good Catholic school
children of St. Ephrem Elementary in a recitation of the Rosary. She
was a tiny lady who had scoliosis and arthritis. At ten, I didn't know
what scoliosis and arthritis were—maybe a pair of Russian hockey
defensemen for the Detroit Red Wings? I just knew she had something
wrong with her. Her back was hunched, she was rail thin, and her
hands resembled tree limbs in the winter. Her digits looked raw and
bony and bent in all directions. She had trouble carrying anything, and
often the Rosary would slide through her hands and fall to the floor.
She would call on a student to pick it up and drape the sacred string
across her gnarled fingers. Naturally she became an easy target for
prepubescent mockery. As she would pray, often with her eyes closed,
my friends and I would bend our fingers into little hooks and laugh.

Originally, I had no intention of including Sister Thomas in this book. She was not a mentor to me. She never gave me sage advice that changed my perspective on the universe. This story does not turn into an episode of *Tuesdays with Tommy*. In fact, I was writing another story when my hand began to throb. As soon as I dropped the pen in pain, her memory rose up like a submarine filling its ballast tanks with air to regain its buoyancy.

Back then, I sarcastically mimicked her. Now she is at the forefront of my memory, and she is standing in an airless classroom under buzzing fluorescent lights. Her nose is sharp and her cheeks are shiny as if she were cut from wax. She is real.

I see myself. I was a ten-year-old boy with a crew cut in a Catholic school uniform: yellow shirt, dark blue tie, and dark blue pants. My feet barely touched the floor. I contorted my hands into claws to the delight of my friends.

I am embarrassed by him. Ashamed. I want to smack the smugness from his face. I want to discipline him. Put him in the corner. Tell him to leave the old nun alone. I want to tell him that in twenty-three years he will stand in front of a classroom full of his own students. That papers will fall from his hands. That his students will chuckle and that he will smile and make a joke to control the moment like he did twenty-three years ago. That although he is standing, he might as well be falling as weightless terror flutters about his chest and while a kindly girl gathers the papers at his feet.

I want to tell him that at thirty-three he will not pray for the mysteries of the Rosary or world peace or for the first pick in his fantasy football draft. I want to tell him that he will pray for his hands. He will pray that his hands may have enough strength to do important things. Like hold his daughter's hand on her wedding day or play catch with his boys on the first day of spring.

I want to look deep into his small blue eyes and tell him many years later, in the late hours of the day under a single lamp light, he will pray that his hands will have enough dexterity to teach his children the things a father wants to teach his children. Like how to make a fist and snap off a punch. How to change a light bulb. Work a screwdriver. Scramble eggs. Shake hands. Write in cursive. Tie shoes. Build a fire. Draw a family of stick figures.

I want to tell this kid to pray for his hands. To pray that his hands may hold on. Because he'll wish those hands could show his children how to lift weights or rake leaves or turn marshmallows over a summer fire. He'll want those same hands to plant tulips in the spring. Carve pumpkins in the fall. Change a tire. Build a fort out of couch cushions so he can crawl inside and make hand puppets by flashlight during a thunderstorm. He'll one day yearn to have those hands tussle hair and flip pancakes on a slow Sunday morning or raise a glass to his children and clap at the echo of their names. That boy doesn't know that those same hands, the ones bent like question marks mocking Sister Thomas as she struggles to move the rosary beads, will one day seize with pain and let go. Of everything.

That boy doesn't know that—twenty-three years later on a cold February morning while his genetic test results rest in a sealed envelope and the world is shifting shades of blue—he'll sit by a window, clench his fists, and cry at the thought of one day being unable to press his hands alongside his children's in wet cement to prove their existence. To prove their aliveness.

THE "GET UP"

I stand up from my seat at the kitchen table, and the motherboard in my head flickers like someone spilled orange juice on it. Blip. Blip. Gravity pulls. I reach for the kitchen table with my left hand as my right arm windmills and windmills and windmills.

Both knees lock then buckle. I'm going down.

I'm stuffed full of our Christmas Day pancake breakfast, but it's happening.

The tendons in my left shoulder—still tender from a fall in September—scream, and I jerk my left hand from the table like it's a hot stove. Blip. Blip. Gravity pulls. My right hand grasps for a wall that's too far. I'm going down.

I turn my head sideways, and my knees, no longer like liquid but bony and hard, piledrive into the kitchen tile. I'm face down on the kitchen floor, holding my breath, staring at pancake crumbs under the table. And it's 2020. Of course it's 2020.

I suspect most of us have never seen ourselves fall. The severity of our fall is measured by the reactions of others. The oohs and ahhs. The shrieks, the gasps, the muted laughter, a wordless evaluation system for the level of embarrassment we should feel right now and for the physical suffering we might feel later. Haley and Chase are somewhere taking inventory of their Christmas presents, and Dylan sits at the table, unblinking, playing the Nintendo Switch Santa had brought him.

"What was that!?" Cindy yells from the kitchen.

"I think Dad just fell," Dylan replies. (I later found out he never took his eyes off his Nintendo.)

I hear footsteps, the electronic jingle of *Mario Kart*, and Frank Sinatra singing "Let It Snow" from the living room speakers.

"Oh my God. Are you okay?"

"I think I'm fine."

"Does anything hurt?"

I want to tell Cindy my pride hurts. My dignity hurts. My self-respect hurts. I feel a million other hurt emotions that can't be seen on an X-ray or MRI. I want to tell her that I'm embarrassed. That I'm afraid the kids will see me and laugh. That one day, she will see me on the ground and come rushing toward my body not out of love, but pity. Pure pity.

I conduct a head-to-toe body scan to see if any areas need immediate medical attention. I run my tongue over my teeth. I sniff. I blink a few times. *Good.* I wiggle my left shoulder. Then my right. *Good.* I shift my weight to my right hip. Then the left. *Good.* There's some throbbing in both knees, but when I flex them the pain doesn't increase. They seem to be okay.

"No, I think I'm good."

"Do you want me to help you up?"

"No. I'm fine. Just let me lie here for a while."

Ataxia is the Greek word for "without order." A few months ago, my doctor called ataxia a "movement disorder." After seven years of living with a hole in my brain, I had never considered the term *movement disorder*. But today, face down on the floor, I do.

Dylan thumbs the Nintendo buttons. Cindy is back in the

kitchen washing dishes. The other kids do not investigate the thud. Frank Sinatra continues to plead with the winter sky.

In 2019, the National Ataxia Foundation appointed me the "Support Group Leader of Philadelphia." In my work, I've met many people who had movement disorders for their entire lives. A lifetime of falling. A lifetime of getting up. I'm always humbled and inspired by their stories and their courage and fortitude to get up and keep going, every day, despite knowing the next fall looms in the not-too-distant future. While I lie on the dirty kitchen floor, I realize the only real movement disorder is failing to get up from whatever pulls us down.

With my right hand, I reach for the edge of the kitchen table and pull myself to my feet again. No one had witnessed my fall. No one witnesses my "get up." No one hears my "get up" but me. So, in a T-shirt and stained sweatpants, I stand up like an invisible suburban superhero with pancake crumbs clinging to my chin.

We all have a private voice in our head. Our private voice is our coach, our narrator, our companion, and maybe our greatest enemy. What we tell ourselves in our difficult, mundane moments will affect the hours, weeks, months, and years that follow. The trajectory of our lives often depends on what the voice inside our head says and the language it uses when we're face down on the kitchen floor.

I know Christmas morning is not the right time to sit the kids down and give them a dad lecture: "Developing your internal voice: How to condition yourself to triumph over hard times." Instead, I'll write this now so that maybe in 2040—when my kids are stressed and frustrated with their adult lives, and they surf the internet for answers—they can read about how their dad fell on the kitchen floor on Christmas morning in 2020, how no one seemed to care, and how he got up.

If something should happen to me, if I should fall and not get up and this book becomes my only way to communicate with my kids in the future, I want them to know that their internal voice is the most powerful thing they will ever own. Do not ignore the power of that voice. Do not let other people's external voice trump your internal one. Just because an external voice is louder than your internal voice doesn't mean it deserves to be listened to. Take time to condition an internal voice that is strong and reliable.

A voice you can trust.

A voice that will help you overcome life's challenges.

A voice that urges you to, "Get up. Grab a broom, and start sweeping."

The kitchen floor is a mess.

MY UPCOMING PHOTO SHOOT (AND WHY YOU SHOULD TAKE A WALK TODAY)

Dr. Readon is concerned about my growing speech difficulties and my recent falls. They indicate growth of the hole in my brain, so he requests that I schedule a brain MRI, which I've come to refer to as a photo shoot. If you've never had a brain MRI, it's usually a painless experience that requires you to lie motionless for thirty minutes in a white tube that resembles a well-lit coffin. The machine's magnetic field serenades you with a symphony of magical jackhammers while computer-generated radio waves take intimate pictures of your brain.

Seven years ago, before my first MRI, I went to a local bar. I put my elbows on the counter and ordered a dark seasonal beer with a high alcohol content. It seemed the right thing to do. Like George Clooney would do as he mulled over how to rob three Las Vegas casinos in one night. My nerves jangled.

My head thumped with worse-case scenarios.

When I had left the bar I wasn't drunk, but I wasn't sober either. I floated in the space between. I had just enough beer in my belly to fall asleep in the bright white coffin, remembering only fragments of the whole experience. Like the exchange with the friendly technician who told me he was from Pakistan and how he and his parents immigrated to America when he was a boy. Like how he jostled my legs when the photo shoot was over. And how when I asked him if I had been snoring, he flicked on the lights and said, "Very much."

This time, I zip up my good jeans, comb my hair, summon my big cheeky smile, and prepare to head to the big city for the photo shoot. I'm not nervous like I was seven years ago. I'm not claustrophobic and, surprisingly, am not bothered by lying in a futuristic coffin. It's more a nervous anticipation this time. Is the hole in my brain getting bigger? Are my recent falls and decline in speech an indication that my disease is getting worse? The photo shoot, COVID, and my pending retirement weigh on me. Thoughts rattle about in my heart and mind. Trap me. Distract me. Steal the power, joy, and optimism I need to get through each day.

Over the winter months, I had developed the habit of walking. In fact, up until this week I had walked forty-six days in a row. Now, we're slammed with a nor'easter. Wind, rain, sleet, and almost a foot of snow slam the area. I stand by the front door bundled up like an eight-year-old kid debating whether I want to go outside. I flip through all the reasons not to go for the walk. It's too cold. It's sleeting. These wool socks and twenty-dollar Walmart boots are already killing my feet. What if I get run off the road by an angry snowplow, pushed into a snowbank, and were lost forever?

Taking a selfie is just another way I procrastinate today's walk.

There's growing research that shows walking outdoors for thirty minutes a day is both physically and mentally healthy. Walking improves mood, increases resilience, calms anxiety, and facilitates creativity. Aristotle, Beethoven, Dickens, Woolf, Einstein, Hemingway, Jobs, and the old lady at the end of my street with the beige bubble coat all would go for regular walks.

Walking offers mental clarity, patience, and some quietude that's hard to find in our noisy modern society. It's a way to finally be alone with your thoughts. For me, walking is not about counting steps or burning calories. It's a way to accept personal responsibility for moving forward. That I'm responsible for my own mental and physical wellness no matter what.

My phone rings. It's an automated reminder for my upcoming photo shoot. I listen, hang up the phone and leave it on the kitchen table, slip on my gloves and my twenty-dollar boots, and thud my way to the front door. If the hole in my brain isn't going to rest, why should I?

I open the door, step into the howling weather, and walk. Like our great geniuses. Like the old lady in the beige bubble coat. One foot in front of the other. Quiet. Keeping my breath. Keeping my pace.

If our family has learned anything recently, it's life is not perfect. There's always going to be illness and social unrest and financial strain. It's always going to snow and rain and hail, and the wind is always going to whip about like an angry jockey. And in spite of all of that, you can always put on your good jeans, comb your hair, and smile. And if you're lucky, you can always go for a walk.

No matter what the MRI results reveal, I'll keep moving forward. Promise me you will too.

DAD, IT'S YOUR TURN TO READ

Chase and I sit on the couch and are about to begin reading *Diary of a Wimpy Kid* out loud. If you're not familiar, the story is about a skinny kid named Greg who records the comical trials and tribulations of being a middle school boy. Parents. Homework. Video games. Gym class. Bullies. Girls. Farts. Earlier in the day, Chase, a middle schooler himself, had his braces removed only to be sentenced to wear a retainer—at all times, except while eating and brushing his teeth, for the next twelve weeks.

"Shhhdad," he says, removing his retainer. "Do I have to wear this thing while I read?"

"That sounds like a mom question."

"MOM!"

A few seconds later Chase returns to the couch, opens his

mouth, and slides in his retainer. "She shed no." (If you don't have a retainer handy and want the full retainer experience, press your tongue to the roof of your mouth and continue reading out loud. Also, make sure you slurp at the end of each paragraph.)

"Sorry, buddy. It's probably good practice anyway."

Chase lowers his eyes, shakes his head, and begins reading, "I sthought I could jus crank ow my shank you cars in a half our but whiting is har work.

(Translation: "I thought I could just crank out my thank-you cards in a half-hour but writing is hard work.")

Halfway down the page, Chase sucks down the saliva that has pooled in his mouth. I stare at him and scrunch my nose as if smelling month-old milk.

He continues, "So I wote a genroll shank you foarm—"

(Translation: "So I wrote a general thank-you form...")

Only nineteen more pages to go.

I taught high school English for seventeen years, and reading was, as you can imagine, a big part of my daily work. Over my career I engaged in various reading strategies with students: silent sustained reading, partner reading, group readings, popcorn readings (when a student reads out loud for a time and then select another student to continue reading from where they stopped). And sometimes, if the text was difficult or needed proper inflection to be fully understood or if I had too much coffee, I would stand on my desk and read out loud to the class like Mr. Keating in *Dead Poets Society*.

Dysarthria (a weakness in speech muscles) is a common problem for people with neurological disorders.

"It's your turn to read, dad."

I clear my throat.

Two sentences and my pace is already too quick. As if late to an appointment, I rush through punctuation and paragraph breaks like stop signs. The words jam and twist and stretch to make one long, strange sound until I gasp like someone who just popped my lungs with a pin.

Chase looks up at me with one-third parts concern, one-third parts empathy, and one-third parts "my dad is sooooo weird."

Slurp.

I take a deep breath, like I'm diving into the deep end of the pool with the cool kids. By the end of the page, I'm pushing out the last words with all the air and effort my lungs can afford until I begin to cough. The visual of a father and son sharing shoulders on the couch reading together on a cold January night is a scene cut from a scrapbook. But the audio of us, slurping and coughing together, is the sound of nightmares.

Between you and me, this attack on my voice is hard to accept. I mean, it's fairly easy to hide a physical weakness. (For one thing, I'm a man. Hiding weaknesses is what we do.) I can lean against a wall or a counter and smile like the almost-handsome middle-aged man I am. But there is no hiding my voice. The slurs. The gasps. The inability to articulate words. The unplanned changes in pitch. Even if I hide in the back corner of the classroom, I'm bound to be called upon.

It's like when a good friend of mine, who I haven't talked to in a few months, called the other day. After we talked family and holidays and politics, he asked, "How are you doing?"

I know he really meant, "How's your health?"

"Physically I feel strong. I'm walking and lifting weights. Getting that beach bod. You know. But it's my voice. It's getting harder for me to speak. Sometimes I sound drunk."

"Are you?"

"I wish. Let me ask you—does my voice sound different?"

"Yes."

Over the years I've accepted the loss of my physical ability, but this one hurts. Like it's personal. Like my disease crossed a line and had the middle school chutzpah to "go there."

I know unhappiness comes from our unwillingness to accept and adapt to our problems. I can't blame my parents, the President (although as I write this on January 6, 2021, blaming my problems on the President is tempting), or my dentist. I must realize I'm responsible for my own life. I'm responsible for how I adapt to change. Because in the end, our willingness or failure to adapt will define us.

Chase slurps through the next page, and I think about how earlier today I had to call the electric company and how the nice woman on the phone asked me three times to repeat myself. And how a friend asked if I'd be interested in doing a guest poetry lesson with some students and I had to explain, via text, "My voice is not up for teaching right now."

Chase reads. It's hard for him. I can hear it and see the strain on his face. Making him read out loud feels like cruel punishment for both of us. Yet he doesn't complain. He's a ten-year-old middle school student becoming aware of his image. Feeling the first tugs of shame and embarrassment. But to live your best life, in middle school and in the years beyond, you have to accept your imperfections. And though accepting yourself might be the hardest thing you ever do, it is the only thing that will bring you lasting happiness.

I must understand the change in my voice is not a punishment. It's simply another symptom that requires adaptation. Like when an orthodontist sticks a wire and rubber contraption into your mouth and says, "I'll see you in twelve weeks."

Chase smiles and slurps at me.

"Shdad, it's you tun to wead."

SPEECH THERAPY

"Mr. Armstrong, you can come back now."

With Clark Able, I follow the speech therapist down a hallway and into a small square room that overlooks the parking garage.

"Hi, I'm Jodie. It's nice to meet you. I've read your chart. You've got a lot going on. How'd did you end up in speech therapy?"

I tell Jodie the story about the hole in my brain, about the falls, and about the difficulty reading aloud. Jodie writes notes on a yellow legal pad. She shakes her head. "That's some story. I need to learn more about your speech. Repeat after me—ZZZZZZZ."

"ZZZZZZZ."

"Good. Ahhhhhhhh."

"Ahhhhhhhh."

"Good. Kakakakakaka."

"Kakakakakaka."

"Good. Now, I'm going to show you a series of pictures on this flip chart, and I want you to tell me what you see."

Jodie draws a line across the yellow legal pad and begins to flip.

"Boy. Car. Star. House. Bathtub. Knife." I lean back and smile.

"I know this is silly," she says, "but there's no adult version of speech therapy. It's the same for kids and adults."

"I feel like I'm in first grade again."

Sensing my frustration, Jodie smiles, "Just a few more."

"Dog. Soap. Duck."

"And what does the duck say?"

"Seriously?"

"Yes."

"Quack."

"Good." She writes something down. "And do you know why ducks quack?"

"—to communicate?"

"Yes. Very good."

Let me be clear. I like Jodie. She's doing a fine job. She's asking questions, taking notes, and establishing a baseline assessment for me. But the "quack" makes me flush with frustration. I'm a forty-year-old man identifying coloring book pictures and quaking like a duck. Throughout my journey I've tried hard not to feel sorry for myself. But, right now, I feel sorry for myself.

A beige and brown tin box, known as the speech trailer, had perched on cinder blocks in my grade school parking lot. Kids would be summoned there by slips of yellow paper. If you were summoned, you'd hope it was in the warm months because the speech trailer had air-conditioning, and the school did not. But, as grade school lore went, the speech trailer didn't have heat. So if you received a yellow slip in February you were encouraged to bring your coat, gloves, hat, and whatever else Mom forced you to wear to school.

I was summoned to the speech trailer once in first grade when going to the speech trailer was still considered mysterious and cool. I identified pictures on laminated index cards (apple, tree, scissors) while a woman wearing big round glasses wrote on a yellow legal tablet. After I identified all of the index cards, big round glasses told me to go back to class. That was the last time I was inside the speech trailer.

Despite the air-conditioning, as you got older, the speech trailer became less cool. That yellow slip announced to everyone something was wrong with you. Now, as I sit in speech therapy as a forty-year-old man, I feel like an eighth grader trying to sneak out of the classroom before anyone notices the yellow slip in his hand. Ashamed. Embarrassed. Emasculated. My self-esteem choking on fumes.

I know I'm not the first person with a neurological disease to struggle with their voice. Yet, in this swirling moment, I feel like I am. Our voice is a part of our identity. Our voice carries our story. Our voice is what makes us distinct and unique and, for better or worse, memorable.

What if I become a stranger to the people who knew me when my voice was clear and boomed like a drum? What if people avoid talking to me? What if I avoid talking to people? What if I'm only seen and no longer heard? What if I lose my ability to teach and tell stories? What if my sarcasm and wit and sincerity remain stuck and unsaid in my head? What if I lose my ability to deliver a well-timed curse word? A punchline? What if I lose my ability to sing off-key? What if I can no longer bullshit with my friends or give a toast at the kids' weddings or tell a story to my grandchildren about their parents? What if I will forever lose my ability to quack with the people I love? What if I lose my voice and then lose myself?

Jodie interrupts my cyclone of worst-case scenarios. "Do you have any questions?"

I take a deep breath, look down at the parking garage iced with snow, and ask, "Given that my disease is progressive, will speech therapy really work? I mean, I'm not trying to—"

She nods, "I know. I understand your fear and skepticism. But, we'll never know until we try."

Jodie's right. We'll never know until we try.

THE MOMENT IN WHICH EVERYTHING IS DIFFERENT

Six days before what had been touted as the most important American presidential election ever, I finish reading Chuck Palahniuk's memoir and writing instruction manual, *Consider This*. Palahniuk, a diesel mechanic turned award-winning author, is best known for penning *Fight Club*, which is a novel that espouses a philosophy of violence. *Consider This* is loaded with practical writing advice. I would recommend it to anyone who has writing aspirations. My single biggest takeaway was a piece of advice Palahniuk received from his mentor, writer Tom Spanbauer, who encouraged him to always write about "the moment in which everything is different."

For writers, this moment in history is fertile ground where good stories can root and sprout. This is the moment of crisis and conflict when characters are at their most valuable to the writer. Because, more than anything, readers crave vulnerable characters.

Readers want to see how a character either overcomes or submits to the new, pressing facts of their lives. And this is writing advice that crosses over into life. The moment in which everything is different is, for better or worse, how we define ourselves.

One of my favorite plays is Shakespeare's *Hamlet*. Yes, the one that is over-analyzed, over-criticized, and often taught poorly in high school English classes. I will not bore you with a summary. I will tell you the entire play hinges on Hamlet's actions after everything becomes different. Hamlet is able to gracefully transcend time and curriculum revisions because at the play's heart there beats the timeless human predicament of deciding what actions to take in a moment when everything is different.

I had started my blog as a way to make sense of the hole my brain. In a way, all the writing I've done since then has been a reaction to that moment when things were different. Does this make me courageous? A hero? God, no. I could easily turn to vodka or meth or various other forms of self-destruction later tonight. So why writing? Because, for some reason which I haven't yet figured out, writing is the substance I depend on to deal with my fate. Because writing has brought order, relief, and joy to that moment after everything was different. Because writing is free and legal. And because writing rarely leaves you with a hangover or lands you in rehab.

But what about you? What about your moments after which everything was different? These are precious moments. Our vulnerable moments are the moments that will define us. What we become is a choice we make at our lowest point. It's not fair. But life is not fair. The actions we take at that critical moment are the most important actions we'll ever take.

A few years ago, I had bumped into a former student. He was taller and skinnier than I remembered. He wore a black T-shirt and black jeans, and the soft flesh inside his elbow was punched with blue holes. He smiled but looked old. Leathery. Deep cracks were carved around his brown eyes. He told me after he had failed out of college he turned to drugs. First painkillers then meth. He said, "It happened so fast."

At two years sober, he was a recovery counselor. He said everyone he met seemed to have similar stories. Something bad happened. People didn't know how to react. So, instead of choosing to deal with their problems, they tried to avoid them with substances. Avoidance just creates more problems to avoid. "I was just like them." He smiled, "But now I help them."

I smiled.

Here was a young man who had destroyed himself in order to find the compassion that now resided in his heart. He reminded me of so many fictional characters I had met in the pages of books. Characters who suffered, learned, and transformed into unforgettable heroes.

We shook hands and parted ways. I haven't seen him since, but I think about him often. He had a presence about him. Like when you meet someone who experienced an earthly horror—a story tattooed with so much pain, so much suffering—only to come back, scarred and smiling, and courageous enough to tell their story.

The day before I wrote this, I drove past an election ballot drop box. With headlights blinking in the rain, a line of cars patiently huffed. The last few months have been hard for the country. And if they've taught us anything, it's that we're a vulnerable nation. A nation with scar spangled lungs. Gasping for air, from sea to shining sea, whispering a national soliloquy, "To be or not to be...," all while wrestling with the tragedy of choice. A choice with consequences. A choice from which everything will be different.

And no matter the choice, for better or worse, it will someday make for a great story.

PS. Haley, Chase, and Dylan. Two things:

1. When you're ready, read *Hamlet* in its entirety. No CliffsNotes. No abridged versions or movies. Be patient. Consider it your admission ticket to joining the confused, complex, and contradictory human race.

2. Vote.

DON'T GIVE UP

Eight years after the phone call that revealed I had *cerebellar atrophy*, I saw a new neurologist—on a friend's recommendation—who specialized in complicated neurological diseases. (It's safe to say all neurological diseases are complicated). The neurologist was cool. He wore a bowtie, asked a lot of questions, took handwritten notes, and made lighthearted neurological disease jokes. He suggested I have a spinal tap to see if my spinal fluid was carrying disease like a roofer up a ladder and into my brain.

White Ladder was the title of David Gray's 1998 best-selling album. I spent many a college night listening to Mr. Gray as I tried to untangle whatever juvenile nonsense I had knotted myself up in. I often think about that eighteen-year-old kid trying to make sense of himself and the world, only to conclude I'm not so different now. Yes, some things are different. I've put on a few pounds. Strobe lights give me headaches. I've replaced cheap light beer with filtered water. But

I'm still listening to "Babylon" on repeat. Still struggling to keep going. I'm still soothed by the music of my youth.

The doctor had straightened his bowtie, scanned his handwritten notes, looked up, and said, "What do we have to lose?"

"I guess nothing," I said. "But does it hurt?"

"Not really."

"Have you had one?"

"A spinal tap? No."

I'm pretty sure in 1998 I spent all of my energy avoiding pain. And when life hurt, I cured myself with cheap light beer and David Gray. Little did I know then, pain is elemental. As long as we're alive, we will never be short on suffering.

My friend Jesse Jackson, Texan host of the Bruce Springsteen podcast *Set Lusting Bruce*, is recording new episodes while he battles his second serious bout with cancer. Trevor, who, like me, has *cerebellar atrophy*, recently reached out from San Diego, California to send positive West Coast vibes to the East Coast. A few weeks ago I got an email from a mother in Ohio whose son had recently been diagnosed with a rare, degenerative neurological disorder. She said she found my blog and thanked me for sharing my story. She said my writing helps her son find hope in a seemingly hopeless time. The nice lady at the end of my street, who waves to me and our dog Maggie May on our morning walks, just had to put down her fourteen-year-old dog.

No matter your affliction, your confusion, your heartache, or your pain, life is hard. Life is really hard. And sometimes I want to quit. Sometimes I want to self-indulge. Sometimes I want pity. Sometimes I don't want to write on. Sometimes I don't want to fight on.

A former student emailed me after a horrible family tragedy to say their life is really hard right now. A lot of tears. A lot of loneliness. A lot of sadness. And then, in the last paragraph, they thanked me for always writing.

Yesterday, I received a message from the cool neurologist regarding my spinal tap. No viruses or stale beer from 1998 had been found in my spinal fluid. The blood tests conducted to find some evidence of why I might have a hole in my brain also came back negative. The neurologist concluded that after eight years of endless and expensive medical tests, the evidence remained unclear. He was still uncertain as to why I have a hole in my brain and, if or when, my condition will worsen.

Let me be clear: I don't want to live like this. I want my balance and vision and speech to return. As much as I love him, I would gladly lean Clark Able in a closest corner forever. I want to ride a bike and run and jump once more. I don't enjoy suffering. I'm not a sadist. I don't enjoy uncertainty. I'm not a Buddhist monk. I'm just a suburban dad who knows my present choices will ripple far into my kids' future lives. Their choices will be, in some way, influenced by my actions. I want them to know, right now, I'm trying my best. I want them to know I endure for them. Because I know one day, when they're struggling in their adult lives, they may ask themselves, "What would Dad do?"

I discover again and again that I'm stronger than my pain. I want you to remember you're stronger than you realize, too.

Don't give up.

Keep going.

What do you have to lose?

BEFORE I TURN OUT THE LIGHTS: LETTER #2

Dear Haley, Chase, and Dylan,

I want you to read poetry. Right now. Before you get old and cranky and consumed by jobs, car insurance rates, supermarket sales, and your kid's soccer practice. You know me as "Dad." But for seventeen years, in three different high schools, they knew me as Mr. Armstrong. The English teacher. And from the feedback I received from the students, parents, and official administrative evaluations, I was an "A minus" teacher.

My classroom desk was often littered with chicken-scratched Post-it notes. I did not decorate my classroom with colorful, motivational decor. For as long as I can remember I had just three black-and-white posters: Mohammed Ali, Bob Dylan, and Bruce Springsteen. I never had a legitimate filing system for student work. Lesson plans were often disorganized and outdated. Classroom novels were haphazardly stacked in a corner, as if the spines were stricken with scoliosis. I failed to keep abreast of the newest advancements in pedagogical theories.

After one particular evaluation, an administrator demanded I stop wasting valuable class time telling personal stories. I told them to "fire me." I was serious. I told them I would rather stock shelves or lay bricks than be denied the opportunity to tell stories to young people. Fortunately, I was not fired. In fact, later that year, I was awarded "The Teacher of the Year" at my school. Sometimes defiance gets a bad rap.

For years I skirted poetry the way you skirt chores. Poetry seemed too hard. Too tedious. Too much risk and not enough reward. Yet, in my last few years of teaching, when my disease had accelerated, I taught more poetry. I found comfort in its mystery. Each poem presented a learning workshop for the students and me.

I assume I avoided teaching poetry for so many years because I didn't want to be wrong. Being vulnerable in public used to bother me. Maybe I just grew comfortable being uncomfortable. When you're the only adult in the room, there's a lot of pressure to be right. When you're older, you'll feel this pressure.

Over seventeen years, a student never announced they planned to go to college and major in poetry. No one said they planned to buy a black beret, a black cat, a black turtleneck, or rent a studio apartment in Brooklyn and chain-smoke all night long.

But many said they planned to keep reading poetry after high school. Even the halfhearted students. They said they liked how poetry comforted them in moments of crisis. When their mom lost her job. When they were rejected by their dream college. When COVID-19 hit. When they watched American cities moan and burn amid the fires of civil unrest in the summer of 2020. Caught in the cross-hairs of history, they said they found shelter in the sturdy verse of a poem.

They even said they never realized how cool poetry was. How defiant poets were. Bukowski. Plath. Thomas. And how anything by e.e. cummings broke enough grammar rules to send an elementary school teacher to the school nurse. How Marvell made them laugh. How Frost inspired them. How Angelou, Hughes, and Dickinson feathered their nerves and thawed their frozen spirit. How poetry made them cry. Wince. Shake. Smile. And think deeply about themselves. About others. And how despite being quarantined in a lifeless town, through a well-written verse they sensed the zipping electricity of the living world just beyond.

They said reading poetry was a way to feel less socially distant. I liked one particular email from a student who said it amazed them how a poet from New Mexico could know how a "seventeen-year-old kid from New Jersey felt." Other students liked how a specific poem, "Good Bones" by Maggie Smith or "Dover Beach" by Matthew Arnold felt. Like an old friend who stood by them when they stood in the street, looking up, convinced the sky was falling.

Like high school, poetry is not a problem to solve. Poetry is proof of existence. Like your portrait in a high school yearbook. You can take a poem at face value and move on or read it like a scientist, trace its features, and wonder about the mysteries hidden just below the surface.

I suspect the world is much, much more than we will ever know. Such is our calamity. We learn so much, yet we know so little. However, we're gifted with teachers who tease out little-by-little, line-by-line the ingredients of the world. Science. Math. History. English. I found a teacher in poetry. A teacher who didn't always understand (with big words, often pretentious rhyme scheme, and obscure allusions to Greek mythology) but who taught me to question, to find humanity in others, and to observe the fine details of fleeting scenery.

Bottom line: Read poetry. You may not become poets but eventually you will have to enroll in the fine art of living. Poems are essential materials for passing the course.For your homework, please read the poems I've assigned below. Prepare an oral presentation of three to five minutes and discuss how the poem relates to your life by connecting it to a personal experience. You must set a minimum of two lines to memory. You will make your presentations after dinner. Also, no PowerPoint. Only halfhearted students use PowerPoint.

Haley, please read "The Journey" by Mary Oliver.

Chase, please read "Golden Retrievals" by Mark Doty.

Dylan, please read "The Voice" by Shel Silverstein.

Goodnight.

I love you.

See you in the morning.

PART II: YOU'RE ONLY YOUNG ONCE

"DAD, WHY IS IT RAINING?"

Dylan and I stare out the window. It's raining hard. The afternoon sky has turned almost purple. Lightning pops, thunder rolls, and a full trash can tumbles weightlessly down the street. His first baseball game is in a few hours.

"Dad, why is it raining?"

"Because it is."

"But why does it rain?"

"Because it's really hot out and the earth needs to cool off."

It's raining harder than it was only a few seconds ago. As if an unseen hand turned an unseen knob to an unseen faucet somewhere between the sun and the moon. The house lights flicker. Someone in another room says, "Uh oh!"

"But Dad, it also rains on cold days."

"You're right buddy. It does."

"So, Dad, why does it rain?"

It's July 2020. We have been quarantined since mid-March. No school and no sports, which for Dylan is 50 percent of his little life. The other 50 percent consists of French toast sticks and sleeping. He has taken the forced change in stride. But here, on the afternoon of his first baseball game, a return to some normalcy is just a crow's hop away. It's dangling in front of him like a Pop-tart on a string. But it's raining on opening day of the in-house-machine-pitch-league season and the little sandlot they play on is now puddled with cats and dogs.

Kids are known for their wild curiosity. It's what makes them interesting. Their relentless questioning is a product of their attempt to make sense of the world. If you hang out with a curious kid, they will pepper you with questions. It's a sort of miracle—you're witnessing them grow up. But somewhere along the way (when they mosey into my twelfth grade English class) questioning is considered a weakness. Silence is fake confidence. A raised hand is subjected to eye rolling.

For fear of embarrassment, we stop asking questions. We condition ourselves to become passive thinkers, declare, "It is what it is," go about our lives, graduate from high school, and grow into adults who complain about the weather. Instead of wanting to know more, we become complacent to know less. Remaining curious—seeing the world through fresh, excited eyes like kids do—is how we stay young, graduate first grade, grow up, and remain cool.

But how do we, the adults in the room, cultivate a habit of curiosity? We have to roll our shoulders back, put our ego aside, admit we know very little about just about everything, and begin to actively pursue life like little kids—wanting to learn, courageous enough to question what we don't understand. And, hopefully, by doing this, we'll finally begin to grow up.

"Dad, do you think my game will be canceled?"

"Probably. I know. It stinks. We wait all these months to play baseball and then, on game day, it rains. It's ironic."

I look at my seven-year-old son. His little chin is on the window ledge. He's staring at the rain. I'm mad. But I don't think he is. He's too curious to be mad.

"Hey, Dad," he looks up at me, smiling with missing teeth and a mouth like a jack-o'-lantern. "What does ironic mean?"

LEARNING TO BREATHE TOGETHER

Chase was born by emergency C-section, and when the doctors hooked, reeled, and fished him out, he wasn't breathing. Hustled like a hot potato to a corner, doctors did what doctors do, and soon his sweet cries filled the operating room, which gave Cindy and me permission to exhale.

We had a boy. A well-fed nine-pound four-ounce beautiful, breathing boy. A boy who walked before he was one. A boy who could hit a pitched baseball at two (I puffed out my chest a little when I wrote that sentence). A boy who, on the eve of his fourth birthday, swallowed a lollipop, turned blue, and went limp in my arms.

Later that day, with his airway cleared and my heart still thumping, Chase and I were walking through the aisles of a store when he asked, with his little, fearless blue eyes, "Dad, can I have another lollipop?"

Chase turned ten this week. He's stretching into a pre-adolescent alien with braces. He's strong and fast and charged with middle-child enthusiasm. Chase breathes excitement into our family. Into the world. Into me.

It terrifies me to know that my innocent boy will soon be at the mercy of the world. The other night, while sitting on the couch watching the terrifying news of the day, a thought struck me—my son turns ten in the same year that, on a Minneapolis street, a last breath started a global revolution. In a year when the whole world seems to be fighting for air.

Stories, with all their alchemy, allow us to recognize each other. To connect to each other. To breathe together in times when air is in short supply. One of the reasons (besides fame and fortune) I often write about my children is that writing these stories is my way of lacing up my high-tops or sliding on the old baseball mitt. It's my way to bump into them. To feel them.

My biggest regret as a father is that I can't play sports with my son. The black hole in my brain has vacuumed out most of my athletic neurons. But Chase is an athlete. Fearless, strong-willed, and eager to defy gravity. Sometimes it's difficult for me to swallow that I can't play one-on-one basketball against him or dare him to hit my fastball. That I can't, with a sweaty brow, breathe hard with him in the backyard on a soft, summer night.

I never felt closer to my father than when we played sports together in the grass and on the blacktop. It created a fellowship, a chemistry, a shared strand of DNA. Skin on skin. Muscle moving atop of muscle. Our lungs working in and out together—like they should. Leaning on each other. Breathing together. Two things the world, and all its colors, need to do right now.

HALEY BECOMES A WRITER

Haley is writing an original story using her spelling words. She works the pencil and finesses the spelling words into a cute story about being a teenage ticket-taker at a roller coaster on a New Jersey shore boardwalk. She's ten and needs her space, so I pretend to look at my phone as I secretly watch her work at the kitchen table, becoming a writer.

Memory mixes with imagination. Muddy thoughts shine like polished stones. The gears and belts and spark plugs of her brain push and pull and let out steam until something happens. Something explodes, like a car key just turned, and her blue eyes fall and her pencil begins to move like a magician twirling her wand. Her mouth draws tight. Her eyes widen. Her right hand tucks some loose strands of blonde hair behind her ear.

The words pour out.

She wills her story into existence.

She's a writer.

The roller coaster chugs up the tracks, hangs, then drops out of sight. A white and gray seagull eats a french fry then scuttles on a pair of toothpick legs across the boardwalk. The roller coaster whips and screams. The smells of salt and sunscreen and funnel cake rise toward the sun, glowing in a sky that is blue and cloudless and forever. Her pencil stops. Her eyes roll upward, to the ceiling, to the heavens like mine do when I can't find the words.

The TV talks.

The boiler runs.

The clock ticks.

Her brain stirs. Her jaw tightens. Electricity strikes and streaks down her chest and bolts into her left hand.

She's writing again and she's a teenager now, leaning on a silver railing that's shining in the fading sunlight. She's wearing white Converse sneakers, and a name tag is pinned on her blue collared shirt. With her blonde hair tucked behind a familiar ear, she's bouncing on her toes, looking for someone. I imagine it's a boy—the one that smiled her way last night. The ocean breaks, the sun sinks, the moon appears, and the roller coaster lights flash. It's getting dark and the boardwalk glows with giddy possibility.

In this sandy stretch of time, new freedoms fool us into thinking that adulthood will never happen and life will always be as breezy as a boardwalk night. Haley finishes writing, closes her imagination, closes her notebook, stands, and walks away. I watch her climb the stairs to her room where she is spending more time now. I should have warned her. Told her imagination is always safer than real life. But I didn't. Because, as a writer, there are some things you simply have to learn on your own.

FATHER-DAUGHTER QUARANTINE PROJECT

Haley is in my writing room when she shouts, "Hey, I remember doing this!" She's found her blackout poem "Two Weeks" while rooting around in my desk.

"Wasn't that a fun project?"

"Yeah, it was."

"I'm thinking some of your poems might just have a place in the book I'm writing."

"Really. That's so cool. Will I be famous?"

"Probably not."

"Oh. It's still cool though."

"Haley, do you know what you were thinking when you wrote them?"

"I don't know."

"No ideas?"

"I just made sure the words I didn't blackout said what I was feeling."

Let's rewind. When the pandemic arrived, I was forced to spend a lot of time with the kids. Not that this is a bad thing; however, the more time I spent with them, the more I realized how much energy it takes to connect with my kids. Especially Haley. Biologically, my sons and I have more in common. And when biology is not enough, we have baseball, ground beef, and fart jokes. But what about Haley? She is quickly cartwheeling into her own fresh-scented, free-of-fart jokes world.

One problem with having taught literature for seventeen years is that certain sentences, like peanut butter, are stuck to the roof of my mouth. Sentences by Hemingway, Fitzgerald, and Shakespeare are sweet and rich and linger long after the nouns and verbs have been digested. And so, when I watched Haley walk down the stairs one morning a few weeks before quarantine had ended, I tasted the first line in Khaled Hosseini's *The Kite Runner*, "I became what I am today at the age of twelve, on a frigid overcast day in the winter of 1975."

Though it was a warm spring morning, the first clause, "I became what I am today at the age of twelve... " stuck to the roof of my mouth. Haley is also twelve, and though she's unaware (aren't we all), she's in the midst of becoming. But the Covid Quarantine of 2020 had exposed the abrupt, declarative nature of our father-daughter interactions.

"Good morning, Haley."

"Good morning, Dad."

"Time to start schoolwork."

"Okay."

"Time to go to bed."

"Okay."

No one warned me that starting a conversation with your kid could be such a terrifying endeavor, especially when your child is suddenly a preteen girl with a cell phone and already skilled at eye rolling. Behind my desire to begin what I hoped would be a lifelong conversation with Haley was a heartfelt desire to be the father she deserves. Selfishly, I want to be the man she will compare all other men to. But this kind of grandiosity has to begin somewhere..

"Haley, what if you and I do a poetry project together?" I said.

"Poetry?"

"Yeah, poetry."

"I don't know anything about poetry."

"That's okay. My students really like when we do blackout poetry. Maybe you and I could do some blackout poems."

"What is blackout poetry?"

"It's when you take a page out of a book and literally blackout certain words, making a poem with the words you didn't blackout."

"Okay."

"Cool."

So Haley and I sat at the kitchen table and flipped through old paperbacks and magazines searching for a page with the right collection of words. Words that could convey what we struggled to communicate if we just exposed them. A low stakes game of communication by elimination. I wanted her to see, firsthand, that even her dad, a writer who spends his days finding words, more often than not struggles to find the right words too. I wanted Haley to know if she begins to articulate her feelings now, when she's older, she will better understand the fruits, or legumes, of communication. And maybe, writer or not, she could author a sentence or two that sticks to the roof of someone's mouth.

"I became what I am today at the age of twelve... " Here are three of Haley's quarantine-inspired blackout poems:

Two Weeks ▬▬

And now, nothing for two weeks. I'm worried ▬▬▬▬▬ ▬▬▬▬▬

▬▬▬▬▬▬▬▬▬▬▬▬▬▬▬▬▬▬▬▬▬▬▬▬

▬▬▬▬▬▬▬▬▬▬▬▬▬▬▬▬▬▬▬▬▬▬▬▬

▬▬▬▬▬▬

▬▬▬▬▬▬▬▬▬▬▬▬▬▬▬▬▬

But ▬▬▬▬▬▬ nothing, ▬▬▬▬▬▬ more and more ag-
itated. ▬▬▬▬▬▬▬▬▬▬▬▬▬▬▬▬▬▬▬▬▬▬

▬▬▬▬▬

▬▬▬▬▬▬▬▬▬▬▬▬▬▬▬▬▬▬▬▬▬▬▬,

▬▬▬▬▬▬▬▬▬▬▬▬ Something must be wrong."
A wave of despair swelled and broke ▬▬▬▬▬▬▬▬

▬▬▬▬▬▬▬▬▬▬▬▬▬▬▬▬▬▬▬▬▬▬▬▬

▬▬▬▬▬▬▬▬▬▬

▬▬▬▬▬▬▬▬▬▬▬ unable to stop ▬▬▬▬▬▬▬▬▬

▬▬▬▬▬▬▬▬▬▬▬▬▬▬▬▬▬▬▬▬▬▬▬▬

▬▬▬▬▬"

▬▬▬▬▬▬▬▬▬▬▬▬▬▬▬▬▬▬▬▬▬▬▬▬

▬▬▬▬▬▬▬▬▬▬▬▬▬▬▬▬▬▬▬

"I'm not wrong," ▬▬▬▬▬▬▬▬ no longer ▬▬▬▬▬▬
▬certain.

▬▬▬▬▬▬▬▬▬▬▬▬▬▬▬▬▬▬▬▬▬▬▬▬

anxiety, ▬▬▬▬▬▬▬▬▬▬▬▬▬▬▬▬▬▬▬▬▬slept
poorly ▬▬▬▬▬▬. Wednesday crawled by. ▬▬▬▬▬▬▬

▬▬▬▬▬▬▬▬▬▬▬▬▬▬▬▬▬▬▬▬▬▬▬▬

▬▬▬▬▬▬▬▬▬▬▬▬▬▬▬▬▬▬▬▬▬▬▬▬.

▬▬▬▬▬▬▬▬▬▬▬▬▬▬▬▬▬▬▬▬▬▬▬▬

▬▬▬▬▬▬▬▬▬▬▬▬▬▬▬▬▬▬▬▬▬▬▬▬

Mom

"_____" Mom _____

·········

Jill _____ for her birthday, _____ phone _____ _____ _____ _____ _____. She's so happy.

_____

I laugh. "_____ knew there was _____"

We play games. _____ pin-the-tail-on-the-hedgehog _____

She keeps talking nonstop. _____

Never-Stops-Talking _____ jill. She's funny _____

·········

_____ games played, cake eaten, _____ feels right. _____

It's Heavier Than You'd Think

I can't even think straight, � it's
▬▬▬▬▬▬▬▬▬▬▬▬▬▬▬▬▬▬▬▬▬▬▬▬

What do I do?
What do I do?
▬▬▬▬▬▬▬▬▬▬▬▬ calming down. ▬▬▬ not
shaking as much ▬▬▬▬▬▬▬▬▬▬▬▬▬▬▬▬
▬▬▬▬▬▬▬▬▬▬▬▬▬▬▬▬▬▬▬▬▬▬▬▬
▬▬▬▬▬▬▬▬▬▬▬▬▬▬▬▬▬▬▬▬▬▬▬▬
▬▬▬▬▬▬▬▬▬▬▬▬▬▬▬▬▬▬▬▬▬▬▬▬
▬▬▬▬
▬▬▬▬▬▬▬▬▬▬▬▬▬▬▬▬▬▬▬▬▬▬▬▬
▬▬▬▬▬▬▬
▬▬▬▬▬▬▬▬▬▬▬▬▬▬▬▬▬▬▬▬ *Can*
you hear me? Can you?
But she ▬▬▬▬▬▬▬▬▬▬▬▬▬▬▬▬▬▬▬
▬▬▬▬▬▬▬▬▬▬▬▬▬▬▬ You just stay
there, okay? You just stay right there."
I take a few more steps ▬▬▬▬ I keep ▬▬▬▬
▬▬▬▬▬▬▬▬▬▬▬ I bring ▬▬▬▬▬▬▬▬
▬▬ I slide ▬▬▬▬▬▬▬▬▬▬▬▬▬▬ I lean
▬▬▬▬▬▬▬▬▬▬▬▬▬▬▬ I keep ▬▬▬▬
▬▬▬▬▬▬▬▬▬▬ I open ▬▬▬▬▬▬▬▬▬

It's heavier than you'd think ▬▬▬▬▬▬▬▬▬
▬▬▬▬▬▬▬▬▬▬▬▬▬▬▬▬▬▬▬▬▬▬▬
▬▬▬▬▬▬▬▬
▬▬▬▬▬▬▬▬
▬▬▬▬▬▬▬▬▬▬▬▬
▬▬▬▬▬▬▬
▬▬▬▬▬▬▬▬▬▬▬▬▬▬▬▬▬▬▬▬▬

In a noisy world, a world that loves to mute intuition, I hope Haley continues the hard work of saying what she is feeling. I see a lot of myself in her. Guarded. Deliberate. Uncertain. We fear people's opinions. We fear our own voice.

This book, especially this chapter, is Haley's reminder that her dad showed her it's okay to say what she is feeling. That it's okay to think before you speak. That it's okay to voice all the poems inside of you.

And because of all that, no other man stands a chance against me.

A LITTLE MORAL COURAGE

Late one night, Cindy and I received an email from Chase's teacher, "I would like to speak to you about Chase." Our rabbit minds had zigzagged through all the ways our son may have broken the rules. Maybe he cheated on a test. Maybe he threw an apple during lunch. Maybe, God forbid, he showed defiance.

The teacher, in a shaky voice, now explains a student threatened to bring a gun to school and shoot everyone—especially anyone who told on him. The teacher clears his throat and says, "Chase was very brave. He did the right thing. Chase spoke up and told a teacher."

When the teacher had talked to Chase, he used the word "sincere." The teacher said Chase's eyes had widened. The teacher asked Chase if he knew what "sincere" meant. When Chase said, "No." The teacher had explained it meant honesty.

If Cindy and I have done anything right as parents, it's that our children know what honesty means. It's a thrill to watch your child do great things. Score a goal, ace a big test, sing a solo in the play, but those accomplishments pale in comparison to when your child displays moral courage when a situation calls for it. When your child speaks up despite knowing the dangers of speaking up. When your child is committed to the truth.

I want Chase to know that not speaking up, moving silently through life, is a long, painful punishment. It's worse than no Xbox for a week or cleaning the bathroom for a month. I know there will be many times in his life when he will not be so brave. When presented with opportunities, Chase may fail to act in good, upstanding ways. I know he is not perfect. He is just as complex and contradictory as any human. I know because I'm still haunted by those times I failed to say or do something—the shame that comes from moral paralysis.

I often write an entry in my blog, hoping that something I say will help someone improve their life. Maybe it does. Maybe it doesn't. But if I'm being honest—I am and have always been writing for my children. In fact, Write On Fight On became a thing only after doctors found a hole in my brain and encouraged me to get my affairs in order. This book is my affair.

So should I die fetching the mail today, my children will know I was a man who, though terribly flawed, had his moments. When life got hard, I tried to find meaning and purpose. I didn't mouse away from the truth. I found strength in helping people. Laughed to avoid self-destruction. Pursued my passion, writing, when it would have been much easier not to. And by writing, I'm urging you—despite fear, despite resistance, despite unwanted attention—to act with moral courage.

Keep up the good work, son.

SEX EDUCATION WITH THE ARMSTRONGS

A few years ago, all five of us stood admiring my newborn niece, Madison Kathleen, as she stirred in her clear hospital-issued bin. My sister-in-law had nodded, smiled, and politely announced it was feeding time.

When I had ushered my three kids out into the white hospital hall, Chase looked up at me with a pair of honest blue eyes and asked, "Dad, how do babies eat?"

Across the hall three nurses leaned elbows-on-a-counter, chatting.

"Excuse me?" I motioned toward them.

They cut their conversation and looked at us.

"Hi. My son would like to know how babies eat?"

They all smiled and one nurse, the most veteran looking of the three, stepped forward and approached us. She leaned down. I stepped aside and Chase nervously smiled. "Well," she scrunched her nose and, with adult seriousness, said, "Babies get their food from their mother's breasts. So with their mouths, babies latch—"

Cindy and I then said our goodbyes and, with our kids trailing behind, we moved down the hospital hall, entered the elevator, took the elevator down to the lobby, crossed the lobby, exited the revolving doors, crossed the breezeway, entered the parking garage, hooked a right, and found our SUV. Before he climbed in, Chase held the door handle. He fixed his eyes on me with the gleam of a boy who had just found a magic key, slipped it into brass hole, turned it, and unlocked the old oak chest that hid all the adult mysteries of the universe. He exclaimed, "So that's what nipples are for!"

Now, Chase and I are driving home from his baseball game. It's a warm March afternoon. There are blue skies, no clouds, and a high sun. It's the kind of day that makes you forget about wearing sunscreen until later when your nose and cheeks and neck are tinted red, and someone tells you that you should've worn sunscreen. The windows were halfway down and the radio is on. Things were going just fine until, from the back seat, Chase asks, "Hey Dad, what is semen?"

I do, what I assume, all unqualified parents do in such situations—I turn up the radio. I whistle. I drum on the steering wheel. I inch down the window a bit more. I keep my eyes locked on the unfurling road ahead. I let the sunshine and ignorance and fear bathe over me.

"Dad?"

I stop whistling and drumming. I hold my breath. Maybe if I stay very still, he will forget about me. About the question.

"Dad. I know you can hear me. What's semen?"

"Um, there's a lot of deer around here. Help me look for deer."

"Dad, is semen a bad word?"

"No, it's not a bad word."

"So what is it?"

I glance at the rearview mirror. Chase stares back at me with a pair of big blue eyes. I wish Cindy was here or Dr. Oz or maybe my high school Phys Ed teacher, Mr. Klebe, with his poster of the male reproductive system to coach me through this answer.

An ancient biochemical reaction stirs inside me. My nervous system releases adrenaline and cortisol. My heart quickens. My muscles tense. My face warms. I can feel the sun burning me now. The logical, mature thing would be to clear my throat and give my son a measured response, but what I want to do is unbuckle the seat belt, toss open the door, jump out, and spend a week in the hospital so that Cindy can answer this one. Before I can calculate the trajectory of a 180-pound man exiting a car traveling east at 40 mph, I'm interrupted again.

"C'mon, Dad tell me."

I should be honest with him. I should tell him I'm a product of semen. So is he. So is Plato, Joan of Arc, Sitting Bull, Thomas Jefferson, Anne Frank, Winston Churchill, President Biden, and Cardi B. No other resource in evolutionary history has shaped the world more than semen. (Except their counterpart, eggs, of course.) The wheel, the Roman Empire, Buddhism, the cotton gin, indoor plumbing, Wrigley Field, and the iPhone would not exist if semen didn't exist.

I should tell him the world is utterly semen dependent. I should tell him that for over three hundred thousand years, semen has been, and remains, one of the most vital currencies in the world.

Humanity's fate hinges on rightful deposits of semen. Without it, the human race faces extinction. I should own up and tell him the truth.

Something inside of me shifts. And so, in a calm, masculine voice, I ask, "Do you want to stop and get something to eat?"

"Daaad—"

Sheer ignorance, the I-spy-deer game, and my attempt to distract him with food are foiled. The kid wants an answer.

With the radio on and the four windows all the way down—a six-cylinder, luxury wind tunnel, I shout, "Semen is—"

"I can't hear you. Can you put up the windows and turn down the radio?"

I listen to my ten-year-old son. I turn down the radio, put up the windows, take a deep breath, and clear my throat.

"Semen is the stuff in your testicles."

"You mean the stuff your balls float in."

"Sure."

He thinks. "Like balloons in a bathtub?"

"Sure."

"Thanks, Dad."

I look into the rearview mirror and Chase is staring out the window. I feel bad. A stronger dad would have told the truth about how babies are born. About semen and ovaries and eggs and sex and storks. This could have been one of those tender father-son moments. The fabled birds and the bees talk. Maybe I can tactfully resuscitate the conversation. Maybe I can rectify my cowardice.

I clear my throat again and say, "Now, let's see if we can find some deer."

DYLAN LEARNS TO RIDE A BIKE

I bet you can tell me when and where you learned to ride a bike. I was five and learned in a white concrete alley behind our red brick Philadelphia row house. The bike was red with black rubber handle grips and solid plastic wheels. A few days earlier, Dad and I had bought the bike from a bearded man with wire-rimmed glasses who sold refurbished bikes from inside his garage.

We probably had similar experiences learning to ride, too. On a warm afternoon, Dad stood behind me. As we eyed the alley, he spoke instructions in my ear. When my feet found the pedals, he held my seat and pushed. I would pedal, and together we found speed. His walk became a trot and the weight of his hand vanished. I pedaled and balanced and glided on my own and, though I couldn't see him, I felt him standing behind, watching the distance grow between us. Then, afraid I had gone too far without him, I kicked my feet off the pedals and scraped them along the concrete until the bike and I stopped. Dad and I repeated the process again and again until I didn't need him anymore.

This week Dylan learned how to ride a bike.

As a parent it's a thrilling moment, witnessing your child learn something permanent like riding a bike. But then comes the quiet moment when they're pedaling away, getting smaller and smaller, and you realize that beneath your pride is a twitch of sadness. You know this is just the beginning of them rushing away to discover new things. Things they won't need you for. Things they won't want you to know about.

But as children, who grew into adults, we always remember learning to ride a bike. It's a moment of independence where we learned we possessed a secret power to achieve previously unknown speeds. It's the closest most of us ever came to flying and with it— giddy possibility. It's a youthful, magical moment where the world became both smaller and larger,and the end of the street didn't seem so far away.

Long may you ride, my son.

CHASE LEARNS THE "F-WORD"

I wasn't ready for it. Not yet. I mean, I knew it would come one day like a thunderstorm or like something I had sent for in the mail. But I just didn't think it would happen on a nondescript morning like this.

But parenthood is funny like that. One moment you're cruising along, one hand on the wheel, window down, sunglasses on and then, like a sucker punch, you're reminded that you're not in control and probably never have been. So with a pair of mangled sunglasses dangling off an ear, you straighten up and attempt to piece together what just happened.

It's Sunday morning. The coffee maker burps, grunts, and beeps. I pour a cup and move to the living room. I park myself on the couch, sip, stare into the glowing face of the laptop, and wait. I wait for the barrel-chested ghost of Ernest Hemingway to appear and inspire me, to remind me that all I have to do is "write one true sentence." Instead of Ernie H., Chase turns the corner sporting glassy eyes, a spiky tuft of bedhead, and his faded green Ninja Turtle pajamas that have been machine-washed too many times. Pajamas that had fit him nicely in June but are now thread-stretched to their limits, forcing the brave Donatello to beg for mercy.

Chase curls up next to me. He rests his head on my shoulder. The TV is off, yet we watch it like it's on. The sun is rising behind me, filling the windows, warming my back.

"Hey, Dad. Do I have a soccer game today?"

"Yes you do, buddy."

"Hey, Dad. Do you think when I'm older I could be a soccer player? Like the kind that plays on TV?"

I tousle his messy hair, smile, and in a hearty dad voice offer my son the most unoriginal dad response I can, "Son, you can be anything you want to be."

Things are perfectly quiet between us, just a father and his son enjoying the company of each other on a slow Sunday morning.

"Hey, Dad?"

"Yes, buddy?'

"Do you know the 'F-word'?"

Pow! Sucker punch. Chew on that, Dad. "Uh, um, uh—.yeah? What—? I mean, do you?"

"Yeah. Fuck. Fuck is the F-word".

I cock my head like a dog hearing his name, hold it there, and wonder. "Bud, where did you learn that?"

"School."

"That's a bad word. We don't say that word."

"Ok, Dad. I won't say it."

But I know he will. I can't expect him to unlearn the word. I didn't. You didn't. The word is now forever buzzing about his brain, like a bee in a jar, waiting for its chance to fly loose and sting his sentences. *Fuck me these pajamas are tight*!

The sun warms the windows and my coffee cools. I hold Chase close feeling that weird mix of hilarity and sadness that is parenthood. Hearing my son, with aggressive bedhead and tight Ninja Turtle pajamas, drop the "F-bomb" is—funny. But I understand its significance. It's gravity and weight. It's a sad indication that the world has sunk its grimy fangs into him, and there is nothing I can do.

Cindy and I police our language around the kids. But here's the scary parental truth: We can only protect, shelter our children for so long. Sooner or later their little bodies will be at the mercy of the world. Yet, as parents, we know that we must send our children off into that tumult—to learn, to discover, to get hurt. Like us, they will be damaged, and they will return home talking dirty. It's just the price we all must pay.

So what do we do when our children learn the "F-word"? Cut out their tongues? Of course not. We can just reinforce that it's a bad word, and if he says it again I will correct him again.

But I can't be naive. By identifying words as "bad" I'm only planting seeds of curiosity. Chase will surely lie in bed at night, further stretching out the Turtles, and wonder what other bad words loom in the darkness where the killer clowns and presidential candidates reside.

Things are quiet. With Chase's head still on my shoulder, I think about how growing up, losing innocence, and vilifying your vocabulary are as natural and normal as the rising sun.

Hey, Dad?

Yeah?

"What do you call a skunk driving a helicopter?"

"What?"

"A smell-a-copter."

I smile, tousle his hair again, and feel the warm reassurance that I'll still have plenty more quiet mornings with my little boy.

PARENTS OF THE YEAR

Haley wants to kill me.

"Dad, seriously. It's like 100 degrees out."

"It's 93."

"It's too hot to do this."

"You're fine."

"I'm a sweaty mess."

"Sweat dries."

Cindy and I are not the "Parents of the Year." We're just as confused, distracted, overwhelmed, and stressed as other parents. Most days we parent on a wing and a prayer and a beer. Most days we feel like frauds.

Some days our children don't shower. Some days they have enough screen time to make a pediatrician tremble. Some days they have Cap'n Crunch for dinner. And some days they go to bed too late because Cindy and I just don't feel like starting the going-to-bed process.

But this summer, for twenty minutes every day for fifty days, we are good parents. On July 8, 2019, Cindy and I had issued our three children a challenge: Practice soccer for twenty minutes a day for fifty straight days. By practice, we meant a twenty-minute supervised session with either Cindy or me.

At first, like they did for any new challenge, my children roared with excitement. There was no nagging, no threatening to "tie your laces and get out there or else." They'd slip on their cleats and rush to the backyard ready to play. But as summer goes on, the mornings grow hotter and more humid. The challenge loses its magic and, like going back to school in September, it becomes something they have to do.

"Dad—," Dylan sniffles and wipes his nose on his shirt, "are we almost done?"

"Crying won't make time go faster."

As the days passed, their challenge had become my challenge. I wanted them to know what it feels like to accomplish a set goal. And if I'm being honest—so did I.

My children saw this challenge as an opportunity to improve their soccer skills, but for Cindy and me, this challenge was about more than just soccer. It was a nook of time, which with busy schedules is hard to find, when we could introduce to and teach our children vital skills like accountability, commitment, humility, and perseverance. Skills that transfer off the playing field and long into life.

The Soccer Challenge at the beach, because training can happen away from home.

"Okay, kids. Today we're working on dribbling with your eyes up."

"It's really buggy out."

"Haley, bugs are only a problem if you let them become a problem."

"Do we have bug spray?"

"No. Now, dribbling with eyes up—"

"Dad?"

"Yes, Dylan?"

"Do gnats have eyes?"

Throughout the soccer challenge I had taken notes, sound bites, of each session. At the conclusion of the challenge, I would compile "Fifty reasons why Mom and Dad made you complete the fifty-day soccer challenge," print it, and hang it by our kitchen table as a reminder of what the challenge taught us and how to face other challenges.

"Be coachable, Chase, and you'll go far."

"Dad, can I go to the bathroom?"

Cindy and I are not the "Parents of the Year." We can be self-prioritizing people, but this summer, for just twenty minutes a day, we are present with our children. We prioritize their improvement. I won't be shy here, and I'll speak for Cindy too, we're proud of our children. They would complete the challenge. They would improve as soccer players and as little people who will go on to face greater challenges in life.

Fifty Reasons Why Mom and Dad Made You Complete the Fifty-day Soccer Challenge

Here is our list of fifty reasons for the soccer challenge. Feel free to share, steal, or use it to start your own challenge:

1. A little practice can go a long way.

2. Accountability matters.

3. Improvement takes effort.

4. Physical exercise is important.

5. Sweat dries.

6. Commitment is an underappreciated quality.

7. Cleaning up is just as important as setting up.

8. We all must do things we don't want to do.

9. Practice is where you grow.

10. Real confidence comes from real work.

11. Don't be afraid to fail.

12. Train in the mornings before your mind tries to convince you not to.

13. Training in the summer heat is possible.

14. Training can happen away from home.

15. We all need encouragement from time to time.

16. Crying doesn't make time go faster.

17. Listening to instructions is appreciated by your parents and your future employers.

18. Appreciate the time you have to play.

19. Practice what makes you uncomfortable.

20. Not every training session will be great.

21. Learn how to compliment a teammate.

22. You will lose.

23. Don't ever quit.

24. Run—even when you're not instructed to.

25. Bugs are only a problem if you let them become a problem.

26. Effort is contagious.

27. Be coachable.

28. Take pride in your improvement.

29. When you're done, put your cleats back where they belong.

30. When it comes to practice: quality over quantity.

31. You will not always be the best.

32. Don't worry about what other people are doing.

33. Focus on your own improvement.

34. Always put your teammate in a position to succeed.

35. Have fun but take your fun seriously.

36. Welcome new challenges.

37. Train like an underdog.

38. Thinking about training is worse than actually training.

39. A positive attitude is a choice. So is a bad one. Choose wisely.

40. Set goals. Reach goals. Repeat.

41. Be humble.

42. Embrace challenges. Don't fear them.

43. We are all a work-in-progress.

44. Improvement happens one day at a time.

45. Don't get angry because someone is better than you.

46. You can only control how hard you work.

47. Like physical strength, mental strength builds from exercise.

48. Take joy in other people's successes.

49. Feeling sorry for yourself will get you nowhere fast.

50. Don't expect perfection.

BEFORE I TURN OUT THE LIGHTS: LETTER # 3

Dear Haley,

Here's a confession: Sometimes I don't know what to say to you. I know it sounds weird. A father unsure of what to say to his daughter, but I have to believe I'm not the only father in the history of fathers, and there have been some bad ones, who has clammed up when faced with the terrifying prospect of talking to his preteen daughter.

I've asked myself: What if I look foolish? What if you roll your eyes and walk away? What if this ends with us yelling at each other? What if I say something that inspires you to shave your eyebrows, get a chainsaw neck tattoo, and form a hardcore metal-punk band called "Death to our Fathers?"

Let me be clear. This has nothing to do with you. This is my inadequacy. My problem to fix. Take the evening of February 4, 2021, for example. It was just you and me at dinner because Mom and the boys were off at baseball practice. Aside from the chewing, slurping, and the occasional knife blade scratching the ceramic plate, dinner was silent.

See, writers are afforded the luxury of imperfection. We can draft, edit, and revise a sentence until the sentence says exactly what we want it to say. Fathers don't have such luxury. I can't spend hours, years, writing multiple drafts of what I want to say to you. By the time I had finally finished, it would be too late. You'd be a grown woman, and I'd be an old coot with gray chin stubble, draped in a flannel robe, mumbling nonsense to myself. Right now, at my computer, I have a thesaurus and spell-check and a worn-out "delete" key. But there, at the dinner table with you, it's just me. Preteen you. Imperfect me.

"So. Did your teacher read your essay about faith?"

"No."

"Oh. I thought it was good."

"Thanks."

"Um, well—" I took a sip of iced tea, set the cup down, and wiped my lips with a napkin. The clouds drifted across the moon. The sun set in Tulsa. Snow swirled in Ontario. Lava bubbled in Bandung. Rain pattered on London roofs. The Indian Ocean swelled and groaned. A cherry blossom quivered, broke apart, and fell on soft green Japanese grass. And I cleared my throat and say, "—yeah, so if you ever want to talk about writing, just ask."

"Ok."

And then we ate in silence.

While I was busy writing this book, the act of writing, like a pair of pure white, fresh-out-the-box Vans, caught your attention. Your teacher assigned you to answer the essay: "What does faith mean to me?" One night, as I was writing, you had asked if I wanted to read it. With one eye on the words, and another eye on you, I recognized a smile. Not my child's smile, but a writer's smile. A smile a writer sneaks covertly when she has written something she is proud of. You wrote:

I am sitting in my classroom, surrounded by teenagers who are slowly drifting away from their faith and God, including myself. As we get older, we are focused on our phones and don't take time out of our day to talk to God. I try my best to pray to God every night and thank him for the gift of life. I pray for my family's and my health and happiness.

Throughout my life, I have learned and gained more information about my father's health. I never really realized that he had incurable diseases until last year. About a month before Christmas, my father had a tumor on the side of his cheek. It was cancerous. I remember praying to God every night until the day he got it removed. Over Christmas break, my family and I would take walks/ runs around the neighborhood. My dad, having health issues, cannot run. My siblings and I cheered him on as he jogged down the street. I kept my faith in him and saw him run for the first time in my life.

When I had finished reading your essay, I cried. And I assume, seeing your reader cry, made you cry too. Reader and writer were crying together. Father and daughter were crying together. It was a beautiful scene and an important writing lesson.

If I could rewind time and return to our dinner on February 4, I would fill the uncomfortable silence with some writing instruction I had learned while writing this book. Since I missed my opportunity, a common theme in everyone's life no matter how confident they appear, I will offer you some of that instruction now in this letter. These are the things I should have told you at dinner:

1. There are two types of writing, private and public. Private writing is for your eyes only: journals, diaries, and memos on your phone. These

are important for helping you clarify what is in your heart and mind. Public writing is meant to be read by a reader. It includes school essays, blogs, emails, novels, children's books, or an angry letter to the Department of Motor Vehicles. The point of public writing is to connect to the reader. A public writer must be selfless. A public writer must attempt to identify, visualize, and connect to their private reader in order to deliver a coherent message.

2. The first draft is always for the writer. Every other draft after is for the reader.

3. Good writing is vulnerable writing. Let your reader hear the things they're reluctant to say out loud by daring to write them down.

4. Young writers often think long sentences mark good writing. Rubbish. Good writing is about communicating clearly. Short sentences show poise and control. They are easily digestible and appreciated by the reader.

5. However, long sentences are sometimes needed to vary the rhythm of a piece, convey a complicated feeling or to show action. Consider the following 142-word sentence in Tim O'Brien's chapter, "The Man I Killed" from *The Things They Carried*. This sentence taught me more about writing than four years of college:

His jaw was in his throat, his upper lip and teeth were gone, his one eye was shut, his other eye was a star-shaped hole, his eyebrows were thin and arched like a woman's, his nose was undamaged, there was a slight tear at the lobe of one ear, his clean black hair was swept upward into a cowlick at the rear of the skull, his forehead was lightly freckled, his fingernails were clean, the skin at his left cheek was peeled back in three ragged strips, his right cheek was smooth and hairless, there was a butterfly on his chin, his neck was open to the spinal cord and the blood there was thick and shiny and it was this wound that had killed him.

Like the narrator, O'Brien wants the reader to feel overwhelmed. To achieve this, he overwhelms the reader with a sheer volume of words. By the time you come to that merciful period, you're dizzy and out of breath and thankful it's over.

6. Get comfortable with contradictions. Humans are contradictory creatures. We value privacy yet we post our lives on the internet. We long for truth yet often lie. We want to know other people's secrets yet fear being exposed. We want awards and prestige yet shrink at hard work. We want to hold on but we yearn to let go. The point is, contradictions are the earthly hub of human conflict. Whether you write fiction or nonfiction, you want to develop characters who—like you and I—are struggling with their own contradictions.

7. Include natural imagery in your writing. As you or your characters live life, gravity pulls, the world turns. Juxtaposing human strife with the grand yet indifferent natural world will stir your reader's imagination and offer them comfort. Because while they are reading your writing, nature is outside their window doing its thing.

8. Include sensory imagery in your writing. Readers want their senses tickled. Describing how something smells, tastes, feels, or sounds helps the reader further appreciate and experience your writing.

9. When you doubt yourself as a writer, take a deep breath, and repeat, "I am a writer" as many times as you need to drive self-doubt away. Also, know that self-doubt never goes away. You can only hope to exile self-doubt to the time-out corner for a brief period. A good rule is one minute of time-out for every year of the writer. For example, a forty-year-old writer should hope to keep self-doubt in time-out for forty minutes.

10. Young writers often measure their writing ability by scores or teacher evaluations. This is a trap, especially if you earn high marks. A good writer knows writing will never be completely mastered or fully understood.

11. Like your room, your first draft should be a mess. Do not capitalize, concern yourself with punctuation, grammar, or proper writing etiquette. Save this tedium for the second and third drafts. Your job with the first draft is to be defiant, dump everything you own on the page and rummage through your stuff until you find what you're looking for.

12. When stuck, go to the supermarket. Maybe it's the neatly arranged produce, the perfectly aligned shelves, the bustle of carts, the buzz of commerce, or the checkerboard floor. When I'm struggling to write, I often wander the supermarket. I know, your dad is so weird. But the supermarket swirls with the stuff of good writing. An urgent journey, sensory imagery, and conflict. Everyone is hunting. And everyone has a desire, a craving, a coupon, and a need to be somewhere else.

13. Have enough confidence to write a poor first draft and enough guts to write a second.

14. Have fun. Write with humor. And remind your reader laughter is essential for survival.

15. The pursuit of perfection leads to procrastination. You or your writing won't be perfect. Get used to it.

16. Start walking. This will help clear your mind and allow for writing breakthroughs you can't achieve while sitting at a computer. Also, walking is a fine metaphor for writing. Go at your own pace, breathe, be patient, and take one step at a time.

17. When you're ready—buy, read, and study the following four books on writing: *Consider This* by Chuck Palahniuk, *Bird by Bird* by Anne Lamott, *On Writing: A Memoir of the Craft* by Stephen King and *The War of Art* by Steven Pressfield. Read with a pen on hand. Highlight and note the parts that strike you as important. Once you finish reading, go write. Reading about writing is helpful, but it will not make you a better writer. Only the act of writing will make you a better writer.

18. A story is only as interesting as its conflict.

19. And finally, as I wrote this book, there were times I rubbed my hands and said, "I can't do this." Ninety-five percent of writing is overcoming those four words. Heck, 95 percent of life is overcoming those four words. You may wonder what the remaining 5 percent is. I don't know. I think it's for us to figure out on our own.

> Good night.
>
> I love you.
>
> See you in the morning.

PART III: YOU'LL UNDERSTAND WHEN YOU'RE OLDER

HOW TO CROSS A THRESHOLD

After reviewing a recent MRI of my brain, Dr. Reardon, my neurologist, informs me that the deterioration that plagued my cerebellum appears to have stopped.

"That can happen?"

"Yes. In some cases, brain atrophy can stop."

"Well, I guess that's good news."

He flashes a smile, leans back in his chair and says, "That's great news. Your brain is showing signs of stability."

A window to a future I once believed in opens: Cindy and I are old, maybe aching with some arthritis, laughing as we watch our grandchildren open their Christmas presents. "So, can I expect my symptoms to improve?"

"Not necessarily. The hole may have ceased atrophying, but unfortunately the damage is done and the symptoms will continue to worsen over time."

"And there's nothing I can do?"

"Physical therapy may keep symptoms at bay for a while, but the symptoms of *cerebellar atrophy* are progressive."

The window slams shut.

The afternoon sun warms the quiet examination room, filters through the window blinds, and slants across the black-and-white tile floor.

Dr. Reardon clears his throat, "Let's do some tests."

He instructs me to follow his finger with my eyes. Touch my nose. Touch his finger. Open my mouth. Stick out my tongue. Cluck my tongue. Snap my fingers. Clack my heels on the floor. Stand up. Sit down. He opens the door, turns and says, "You know the drill."

I stand up and follow him out into the hallway. I walk to the end of the hall, arms by my side, make a controlled turn—as if trying to earn for my driver's permit—and walk back to him.

"Your gait looks good. You're walking more confidently than you have in years."

"Thanks."

We move back into his office and sit down. He picks up a microphone that is corded to his computer and begins dictating the results of my tests. "Despite extensive cerebellum damage, the patient's gait has shown improvement—."

I comment how when I first met him, four years ago, he had to scribble down test results and appointment notes by hand.

He smiles, "Yes, this will definitely stave off carpal tunnel for a few more years. But to be honest, I miss the old-fashioned thrill of physical note-taking. But, things change. Do you have any other questions?"

"I do. This may sound weird. I get a little uneasy around thresholds and doorways. You know, like I'm afraid to transition or something. Is it normal for people with cerebellar damage to have trouble crossing thresholds?"

He leans back into his seat again, crosses his legs, and explains that the brain is a wonderful mystery. Even a healthy brain can find thresholds problematic. It's something primitive. Like the fear the primitive man must have felt while standing barefoot on some rocky ledge, looking for someplace to go. Crossing from room to room, from one plane to the next has always troubled people. Evolution has ingrained it in our psyche. We're simply afraid of transitions.

"Do you have any advice on how to cross a threshold?"

"Crossing a threshold is often mental. The initial fear of just transitioning from one place to the next often prevents us from progression. But when you find the nerve to finally cross, you realize there was nothing to fear at all."

I stand up, shake his hand, and say I'm looking forward to seeing him in six months. He smiles, spins away, opens the door, and disappears. I slip on my coat and stride through the threshold from the examination room into the hall and back into life.

A life born of thresholds, waiting patiently for me to simply shore up the courage and cross.

THE WINK

My experience as a teacher has led me to believe that eighth-grade boys are the most repulsive things on the planet. They're gangly looking aliens that smell like wet dreams. They grow out of clothes quicker than you can say "skinny jeans," and they eat a week's worth of food for dinner and never put on weight. These conceited assholes make no contribution to the goodness of humankind aside from having coasted up Middle School Mountain, which should prohibit their right to be narcissists or assholes.

As an eighth grader, I was five feet, four inches, and ninety pounds. I hadn't hit puberty or kissed a girl. While most of my classmates spent their weekends dry humping, my Saturday nights featured Nerf battles with my friend Dan and a few other undeveloped tadpoles. I learned about high school from the kids of *90210*. Aaron Spelling's fantasy made me believe that all high school fellas had goatees and muscles, drove convertibles, and had unprotected sex with their pouty-lipped girlfriends in the Peach Pit bathroom. So naturally I spent most of eighth grade scared to death.

I watched boys mutate into men. Strange-looking gremlins with crackling voices and patches of facial hair. To my amazement, I watched girl after girl give herself up to these strange things. Eighth-grade girls wanted to make out with boys who looked like men. They wanted their virgin cheeks rubbed by sharp facial stubble. They didn't want to kiss their little brother. At fourteen, that's what I looked like— America's favorite little brother. Parted hair. Freckles. High pitched little boy voice. And more insecurities than pubic hair.

The one equalizer was my athletic ability. Though I was small and weak, I was fast and agile. Sports earned me a thread of respectability. But I knew soon I would be sharing high school halls with Dylan McKay and Brandon Walsh, and I would be pulverized into a pile of pubescent dust.

Then this happened.

A May evening. A sinking sun. A gold sky that stretched like a lion's fleece. Under the tutelage of my dad and his best friend Coach Turner, the St. Ephrem's varsity baseball team found itself in a precarious position. We had bullied our way through the regular season and were one game away from an undefeated record. However, on this night, in the championship game, we found ourselves tied four to four in the bottom of the seventh to the cross-town rivals, Queen of the Universe. I was due to lead off the bottom of the seventh inning.

Because of my lack of size and strength, batting was a problem. My weapon of choice was the same thin barreled bat I used in sixth grade, not for bat speed but because my twigs couldn't handle anything else. And for your baseball purists out there who are thinking, "Why not bunt?" Three reasons: Most teams brought the infield in on my sheer lack of size. My bat barrel was so thin that the margin for error was narrow. I had an absolute fear of getting my fat little fingers crushed by a fastball.

Please don't think I was on the team because Dad was the coach. I may be selling myself a bit short on my baseball abilities since my game had some redeeming qualities. I was an above-average fielder with a solid baseball IQ, and because of my speed, I could be a terror on the base path. However, I simply could not hit. The scouting report on my approach at the plate went in this order: Looks to get walked. Gets hit by a pitch. Prays and swings.

I stood on the edge of the infield grass, scared out of my Nike cleats, watching the pitcher rear back and throw a few warm-up pitches. He looked like most of the kids I feared. Tall and lanky with a square jaw, a spotty goatee, and sideburns. Stalking the mound with the confidence of a man that spent his weekends dry humping.

Eighth grade was difficult for me because only three years prior, in fifth grade, I ran with the "in" crowd. Before the puberty epidemic, which I seemed immune to, life had been good. In fact, I was one-half of the first "relationship" in my grade. Her name was Courtney. She had brown spiraled hair. We never got beyond holding hands at the skating parties and passing notes in class, but I established in fifth grade that I could get girls without really doing anything. This is how our relationship began:

Courtney's friend Jen said, "Courtney likes you. Do you want to go out with her?"

I replied, "Sure."

"Congratulations. You're a couple."

And two months later, this is how the relationship ended:

Jen said, "Courtney doesn't want to go out with you."

I said, "Ok."

"Sorry. You're not a couple anymore."

The umpire barked, "Batter up!" I crossed home plate and eyed down the third-base line to Coach Turner. Married to a professional cheerleader, Coach Turner was the closest thing I knew to a chain-smoking pirate. He walked with a limp and sported a seafaring scowl that would make a sailor's asshole pucker. Coach Turner's meaty left hand had tugged at the bill of his cap while his right hand ran down his thigh, signaling that I was to "take" the first pitch. I stepped into the batter box, screwing my back foot into the dirt.

The first pitch sizzled in—a belt-high fastball that popped into the catcher's mitt.

"Strike one!"

I had stepped out of the batter's box and looked down the third baseline. Coach Turner put his hands on his hips and drilled holes through me with his eyes. I knew that look well. He was telling me I should pray and swing, but he was secretly hoping I'd take a fastball in the ribs. I turned toward the batter's box. I felt Dad's presence looming in foul territory by the first base bag some ninety feet away. At that moment I felt embarrassed for Dad. The coach's son, scared to swing.

I stepped into the batter's box. I wrung the bat handle. A second belt-high fastball whistled in.

"Strike two!"

The Queen players erupted in jeers, "One more! He's afraid to swing!"

I stepped out of the batter's box and looked down at Coach Turner. There were two strikes. Bottom of the seventh. Tie game. There was no signal for "Stop being a coward and swing the fucking bat," so he spread his arms out, palms face up in disgust. The reaction a pirate would give when questioned by an IRS agent about pillaged loot.

I must have looked foolish to Coach Turner. A little boy in a baseball uniform just circling the drain of life. Before I stepped back into the batter's box, I looked toward Dad who stood in foul territory, patrolling first base.

Unlike Coach Turner, Dad was a modest man. Always calm. Never swept up by emotions or the magnitude of the moment. Then and now Dad is the Zeus in my mythology. He's all powerful. All knowing. In a good way. Not in that prickish—I'm your father, the ruler of the universe, and you will do as I command—way. Dad had quiet determination. He had graduated from high school and immediately went to work as a welder. He later went on to open his own business repairing and selling pallets.

At the height of the evening's drama, Dad looked down the

first base line and into my soul. The sun sank behind the tree line. Crickets hummed. Fingers were crossed. All those eyes were locked on me. The players, the crowd, the entire cast of *90210*. A swirl of voices screamed and whooped, cheered and jeered.

I felt myself collapsing under the weight of my adolescence. Failing at fourteen, on this stage, would be cataclysmic and undoubtedly cost my parents years of therapy co-pays. Dad knelt and ran his hand across the points of grass. Then, as subtle as the advent of the moon and as natural as the setting sun, he winked at me.

I climbed back into the batter's box, choked up on the bat, and shortened my stance. Just like Dad had taught me. The pitcher reared back. The ball shot off the bat and rolled toward the dead space between the pitcher's mound and first base. I dropped the bat and tore down the first base line. The first baseman retreated to the base. The pitcher leaped off the mound. Dad still knelt. The sun was at his back as he helplessly watched his son struggle in a world full of giants.

"Safe!"

The evening sky erupted in a burst of cheers and moans. Dad moved in behind me, put his hand on the small of my back, and calmly said, "Check your signs."

I looked across the infield. The pirate ran his right hand

down his left sleeve. Steal. On the next pitch I took off for second.

"Safe!"

Brian, the best hitter on our team and a seventh grader who had hit puberty, sent the next pitch flying out to right-center. I sprinted toward third. The pirate hopped up and down waving me home.Things were quiet in the car. Every so often Dad and I looked at each other and smiled. Still speaking in signals. Like father and son so often do. As we rounded the corner and headed home, I asked, "Dad, why did you wink at me?"

I felt the weight of the championship trophy in my hands. The sky shifted into deep purple. Single suburban houses with yellow porch lights flickered by. Dad looked across the car and said, "Because I believe in you."

We slid into the driveway. Safe from the scrutiny of the world. Dad cut the engine and I looked over at him and his eyes met mine. "Thanks, Dad."

Fast forward to 2020. There are many nights when I convince myself this book will never happen. When I fall into myself and teeter on the edge of failure. When I think it won't be worth the work. When my kids pine for attention or when I can't muster the energy to find a single word that satisfies me. When the blank Word document is as menacing as a strapping pitcher with facial hair and a propensity for destroying twerps like me.

Sometimes I fail. Sometimes I don't swing.

Then sometimes I see a baby-faced fourteen-year-old boy in baggy blue baseball pants standing in the on-deck circle. His head rattles about in an oversized helmet. He's scared out of his skull. Scared of everything. And I see my father. He's a young man. Strong. Proud. With the sun behind him, he kneels in the green grass and winks at me the way fathers do who secretly believe in their sons.

Then the pitch comes.

And I'm scared.

But I swing.

Every time.

Dad and me after the game. Circa 1994.

THE GOOD CANCER

Ready or not, life happens at breakneck speed all around us, and it's our responsibility to decide what to do with it. Our happiness, our ability to make lemonade, comes down to perspective. I write these sentences a few days before Christmas, just a few weeks before 2019 becomes 2020, and just a few months before the world will stand still in the face of global pandemic. Haley interrupts to ask me to help her study subject-verb complements for a test. Dylan springs into the once quiet living room and begins wrestling with a couch cushion. I can hear Cindy hustling down the stairs. She calls out to no one in particular, "The vacuum is broken!"

My train of thought is broken, and my phone rings. The voice on the other end tells me I have cancer. Basal cell carcinoma. Skin cancer. The good cancer. It's just above my left jaw line, below my ear. Ready or not, cancer or not.

Have you ever been given bad news and asked yourself, "Why me?" Have you ever tossed your hands up and said, "If it weren't for bad luck, I wouldn't have any luck at all?" Have you ever shaken your head and said, "It's just not fair?" I find myself doing a lot of that now. I'm holding some ugly-sweater pity parties for myself. Be thankful you are not invited. But I just can't think of doing anything short of wallowing. I don't want to contrive positive vibes if I have none. And these days, it seems there's enough wallowing at work, at the crowded food store, in the frozen mall parking lot to stuff our stockings. When I heard the doctor's diagnosis, even though he said it was "the good cancer"—common, treatable—I can't help but think here we go again. Another worry. Another illness. Another lump of coal.

On Christmas Eve, just a few days later, I have a four-hour procedure to remove the cancer cells. My doctor is fairly certain things will be fine. Some soreness, some stitches, but nothing that might infringe on Christmas plans. Maybe I overreacted, but when you hear you have cancer, even the good cancer, I guess it's normal to take a long drink from the short glass of self-pity.

I don't need to remind you that life is hard. Life is full of worry and despair and anger and frustration and sadness. There are high and lows and valleys of uncertainty in-between. I know. From Dr. Thomas's phone call in 2013 to the uncertainty of today, for almost a decade, I have traversed those emotions. I have lost my footing, and I'm in desperate need of a guide.

When we're tramping through hard times, we tend to think we tramp alone. That no one understands our journey. That our burden rests uniquely on our shoulders. That our burden is solely ours to carry. The purpose of my writing is not for pretentious soapbox pontification or to tell you how to live your life or to make you think I'm some suburban doyen sitting high in his seven-passenger minivan disguised as an SUV.

I'm writing to remind myself to write on and fight on. I'm writing so that you and I may feel less alone. I'm writing so that you and I may recognize that our setbacks are ripe opportunities to embrace new and fruitful perspectives. As a friend recovering from drug addiction once said to me, "I had to eat shit in order to know what real food tastes like."

Sure, you may eat alone, but you don't suffer alone. We do not experience life alone. Our ups and downs are shared by others. Acknowledging your suffering, your behavior, is negatively affecting the people you love, the people you want positive things for, is your cue to change your perspective.

Stories drive us. I believe we begin to understand mysterious parts of ourselves when we witness those parts working the engine of someone else's life—a minivan that appears to be running a little smoother than ours. Personal attitudes, definitions, and perspectives only shift when we let other people's stories turn the key and ignite our own engine.

I can't tell you how to live your life. I can't tell you everything is going to be okay. But I can tell you a story. I can tell you that I have cancer. The good cancer.

THE WORKING MAN RETIRES

"I love my father." There, I said it. Four words that sons too often hide from their fathers. Why? Fear of rejection. Fear of embarrassment. The awkwardness of man-to-man communication. My love wells up from knowing what my father has endured. For fifty-plus years, he did something so unremarkable, something so pedestrian that, in time, it will be forgotten—he went to work.

On April 3, 2020, my father officially retired from his working life. Because of COVID-19, there were no standing ovations, no pats on the back, no handshakes, no steak dinner, no beers at the bar, no four-wheel ride off into the suburban sunset. Sadly, in the modest words of my favorite poet, T.S. Eliot, my father retired "Not with a bang but a whimper." Which, when considering the totality of his working life, makes perfect sense.

A physically able, lunch-pail carrying kid, my father grew up into a man among the sharp steel and diesel smells of factories and warehouses and tin trailers that immortalize industrial America. Unforgiving summers. Relentless winters. Crowbars. Safety goggles. Cowhide gloves. Industrial fans. Propane heaters. My father's working life and mine are very different: the imagery, the uniform, the instruments of our deliverance. He turned wrenches. I turn pens. He wore steel-toed boots. I wear loafers. His hands hardened with calluses and were stained with grease. I have paper cuts and ink smudges.

For a while, these differences worried me. These differences jabbed at my own masculine insecurities. Like Nick Carraway expressed in the first sentence of Fitzgerald's *The Great Gatsby* ("In my younger, more vulnerable years..."), I foolishly wondered if my father was proud of my workingman life. Was he proud his oldest son was a teacher and a writer who could weld words but didn't belong anywhere near a blowtorch?

Dad and me at work. Circa 1984.

Growing up, my father would often tell me, "Use your brain and not your body." I'm older now, owner of a broken body myself, and enmeshed in my working life. I realize, with deeper gravity, what he meant. The working life comes with a cost. You pay tolls, certainly with your spirit, but also with your body or your mind—or sometimes both.

My father paid with his body. Not that he didn't use his mind. He did. In fact, I consider him one of the smartest people I know. But his work was almost always physical. His body, his most effective tool, over time, began to rust like a wrench left in the rain.

I now realize it's not the type of work but how I perform the work that matters. Put simply, did I give my best effort to each workday? Sure, I'm not building trusses, but I tongue and groove sentences together until those sentences form a paragraph and that paragraph joins another paragraph. Soon I have an essay or a post or a story. Soon I have something I crafted into a brick-and-mortar existence. Soon I have something I can walk inside, run my hand across the walls, breathe in the dust and sweat, and admire.

I also realize that though we wear different uniforms, my father and I are both repairmen. We have different tools, different trades. He cleared clogged drains and replaced broken windows while

I renovate grammar and syntax and rectify pesky literary matters.

Now that it has come to pass, I understand my father's working life was never about a paycheck. Maybe no father's working life really is. Maybe it's about the impressions you leave on your children, the attitudes you instill in them about work. But, of course, I failed to understand this when I was busy teaching. Sure, his paycheck provided my brothers and me with a soft, suburban life, clothes from the Gap, and higher education. But, beyond the thin monetary rewards of his job, my father's working life thankfully ingrained in me a persistence I now attempt to carry forward to every blank page and that I hope to, one day, gift to my children.

I want my father to know his commitment to a working life awakens every time I open the computer and begin building sentences, piece by piece, the way he built the shed in the backyard one summer when I was a kid. Sun at his back, hammer in hand, persistence in his heart. Now, every time I teach a lesson or write a story, I look at the image blazed upon my own heart of a working man and see my father.

THE PLAN

We often enter adulthood with a plan. Maybe it's hashed out over a cup of coffee or maybe a shot or two of tequila. Nonetheless, we were once pie-eyed dreamers standing at our threshold, staring out into the future, and sketching a map that appeared direct and seamless and promised us the life we thought we desired and deserved.

A few months before I met Dr. Simon, I rolled up my sleeves and went to work on my plan. A plan that made professional and financial sense. A plan that was, in my opinion, neat and uniform, and while perhaps a bit boring, a plan that made sense. So in January 2013, I enrolled in grad school to earn a master's degree in educational administration, a move that could score a principal job and an office with a bathroom and a secretary to field my phone calls and fetch my coffee. When I shared my plan, people smiled, nodded, raised a glass, and congratulated me on my initiative. The praise and support felt good. It was seductive and reassuring. Yet underneath my smile and my thin, freckled face, fear and uncertainty brewed.

I could feel myself falling into a professional life I didn't want. I was allowing money and the tempting thoughts of a mahogany desk and a gold-plated plaque with my name engraved on it to guide my compass. And in my pursuit of such frivolous things, I ignored the pull of passion. I ignored that internal voice, the one we all have, the one we're quick to dismiss, as I turned toward the thing that I despised the most: the inauthentic.

I should have known, when I was willing to invest money but not time, that I was chasing down someone else's dream. I should have known when I wanted the rewards without the work. I should have known when the voice inside was screaming, "No!" But like I said, this plan made sense.

Have you ever told a lie, then convinced yourself it was the truth?

I have.

That's what grad school was like for me. I told people it was what I wanted when it wasn't. It was like staying in a relationship you no longer believed in. I guess I stayed committed because it was safe. It was never a matter of love or passion. It was a matter of uniformity. It was the most inauthentic stretch of time in my life.

If you have stayed with me this far in the book, it's time you know something: I consider myself lucky. If I had never received the phone call, if my brain had remained normal, I probably would have earned my degree, become a school principal, and never gotten around to writing this sentence.

Yes, my bank account would probably be bigger, but would I honor and celebrate the fleeting nature of time and energy the way I do now? And yes, I would have my health, but what about self-respect? What about passion? What about the authenticity I seek?

A few months after Danny drew a turd on my classroom whiteboard, I dropped out of grad school. I was three classes away from earning a degree in educational administration. Many people asked why I dropped out. Why didn't I just tough it out and finish? Because the fact remains, I woke up this morning with a hole in my brain. I will wake up tomorrow with a hole in my brain. Because spending money, time, and energy on something I'm not passionate about will not fill the hole in my brain.

WHY YOU SHOULD READ *THE ALCHEMIST* WHEN YOU'RE OLDER

If I could have a conversation with my thirty-year-old self, it would go like this:

"It's called *The Alchemist* and you should read it."

"Why?"

"Because you're thirty. Because you're foolish. Because you're playing it safe. Because you think time is your friend. You yearn for the wrong things. You make halfhearted choices. You feel obligated to adopt people's opinions as your truth because you desperately fear rejection. You want to live the easy life but expect rewards that require hard work. You take too much for granted. You've failed to understand that all choices, even the small ones, ripple with consequences. Even choosing not to choose has consequences. You should read *The Alchemist* because you're going to father two more children, and you're going to invest your money in grad school. Then you're going to get sick, chronically ill, with a sickness that will break you physically and test you spiritually."

You might just gape at me at this point.

But I'd continue, "On a cold December day, you'll wring your hands and look into the soft eyes of your children and shut your laptop. You'll drop out of grad school and be more lost than you've ever been. And it's only then, as you wade through some of the most draining, exhausting, terrifying hours, days, weeks, months, and years that you'll learn pain is necessary for growth. That your scars, those jagged stories, knitted with conflict that tattoo your limbs and your internal organs are signs, are omens from a higher power that give your life meaning and purpose."

My thirty-year old self would look down, kick dust for a while, and as if talking to his toes would ask "What's the book again?"

"*The Alchemist* by Paulo Coelho. He's Brazilian."

The silence would balloon into something big and palpable between us. My younger self would turn up his eyes and offer that familiar, coy smile only found in photo albums now. He's young and thin and clueless. "So, this Alchemist book—," he'd cross his arms and lean his shoulders back, "—can I get the SparkNotes?"

In the preface to the anniversary edition, the author describes how *The Alchemist* sold only one copy in the first week. A second copy sold six months later—to the same person! Within a year, more than sixty-five million copies were sold in eighty different languages, a Guinness Record for most translated book by a living author.

The premise of *The Alchemist* is simple: An impoverished sheep herder, Santiago, decides to sell his flock to go questing across the Arabic desert for a treasure supposedly located near the Pyramids of Egypt. Of course, what he learns about himself, about life, and happiness and love and truth on the journey are more valuable than any extravagant treasure he could find.

Why am I such a fan? Because Coelho implores a very simple, parable style to tell Santiago's story, which is essentially the story of humankind. It's about decision-making. It's about following your dreams. It's about choosing to live a life that gives your heart and soul meaning and purpose. It's about finding your true self, or as Coelho calls it, "Personal Legend."

Making a decision and living with the consequences is super hard. I always thought the older and more mature I got the easier decision-making would be. Not true. In fact, I'm learning the older you get the more variables there are (money, children, health, job security) and the harder decisions become. As adults, we fear being wrong. We yearn to make the perfect decision. We foolishly think the right decision will unlock a magical unicorn life.

The Alchemist argues that we can live a good life by avoiding decision-making and risk-taking. We can earn money, own a house, raise a family, make friends, and host parties. We can have all the comforts of a "good life" like we see in magazine advertising. However, the "good life" will always fall short of the one we imagined for ourselves.

This "good life," the cautious life, will always prevent us from achieving our Personal Legend. And this "good life" will gnaw at us, dog us, press us, and leave us with a hollow heart that beats and beats and beats as we stagger through a desert filled life, a life that mercifully ends with our inevitable death. *The Alchemist* reminds us that the easy path, the lighted and well-worn path traversed by so many souls, is the far more dangerous path than the mysterious, untrodden path.

Life is a noisy ride. Whether we're ready for it or not, we will hear everyone's opinions about ourselves and what we are doing with our lives. If we adopt what others think of us as our truths, we will come to hate ourselves. We will live, as American philosopher Henry David Thoreau described, "a life of quiet desperation." *The Alchemist*'s narrative style amplifies the book's simple message: No matter the noise, no matter the costs—follow your destiny.

Five more reasons to read *The Alchemist*:

1. Every human learns of their destiny as a child. As a child we play, we embrace our passions. However, we age and the world's opinions infiltrate our hearts. We abandon our destiny and replace what we really want with what other people want for us.

2. We must be aware of signs/omens. They offer clarity and direction.

3. Our choices have consequences that stretch beyond our knowledge and our lifetime.

4. Our destiny, our ultimate goal, requires endless suffering.

5. Suffering for our destiny is more heroic, more rewarding, and all-around more badass than living a safe life.

A GOOD MOMENT (IN A YEAR OF BAD MOMENTS)

Some things I write are, by definition, stories. They have a beginning, middle, and end. Rising action. Falling action. They have character arcs and conflicts. They have resolutions and themes. The stories I write are true. Or as close to true as my flawed memory and limited perspective allow them to be. I write stories about my life, so five or twenty-five or fifty years from now, when I'm dead, my children can learn about me as if they're in history class and the teacher just instructed them to open their books to the chapter entitled, "Abraham Lincoln."

Not that I'm comparing myself to Lincoln. His story is far more compelling than mine. Not more important. Just more compelling. A more meaningful drama—with the war and slavery and the Gettysburg Address and all. My story, as a New Jersey high school English teacher struggling to do his best with a neurological disease, doesn't come close to Abraham Lincoln's story and the historical impact his life had and continues to have. However, I've got to believe, as we celebrate Lincoln's life in movies and biographies, there were many things about Lincoln the father or Lincoln the husband we never learned about. Many small moments that were just as important to him as anything printed in the pages of school textbooks.

Parents will certainly remember moments their children will forget. Like when a child, probably sitting in a highchair, is given a plate of spaghetti topped with tomato sauce for the first time and how that child dumped the plate on their head and laughed because everyone at the table laughed. If stimulating a reaction is, for better or worse, a connection, the child just learned a valuable lesson. Partly from age and partly from a worsening of my condition, I'm beginning to think it's my fatherly duty to record and keep alive the small moments before the phone rings or another birthday is celebrated, or my children are accepted into their dream college and move out, and before those little moments that lives are built on evaporate forever.

This entry isn't a story. It might not even be an anecdote. It's just a simple happening. A moment that means a lot to me and hopefully will mean something to Chase when he's older. A moment that, if I don't write it down, will surely be a forgotten moment in a life of mostly forgotten moments.

It goes like this: I'm sitting at the kitchen table staring at my laptop, attempting to grade student essays. After a few hours of staring at the screen, my nystagmus, a symptom of the *cerebellar atrophy* that makes my eyes bounce like rubber balls in their bony sockets, seems to have guzzled a Red Bull. I hold the laptop slightly above my eyes and look up at the screen. This helps. Maybe it's the angle but my eyes settle and I can read, but with both hands holding the laptop I can't type. The amount of screen time remote teaching requires strains and aggravates my already troubled eyes. I'm worried (or at least pretend to be) about my kids' screen time. But what about mine?

Anyway, the front door creaks open and slams shut. I'm holding the laptop level with my eyes. I'm concentrating on the words. I don't know which child just went outside. Or why.

The door swings back open.

"Dad, come quick!" Chase's voice booms and the door slams shut again.

I glance over to him, and let out a sigh. "I'll be right there."

I set the laptop on the table, take a deep breath, rub my eyes, push up from the table, move to the door, open the door, and find Chase standing on the front step.

He looks at me and points up.

"Dad, look at the sky. It looks like cotton candy."

And together we stare at the sky. It's a nice moment. Quiet. Easy on the eyes. Did Lincoln have these moments with any of his children? Did he ever regret the time spent away from home? Away from his kids? Did being president of a country embroiled in a civil war compromise his fatherly devotion like how being a high school English teacher strapped with essays compromises mine?

One day I will not be here to look up at the cotton candy sky with my son. And maybe, many years from now, after he graduates from Princeton University and is elected the President of the United States, and after he saves the country from some national crisis, he will be invited to balcony seats at the theater. Maybe to see a reprise of *Hamilton*. Unlike Lincoln, he'll decline the invitation and, if history is a good predictor, his disinclination will save his life. He will elect to stay home at the White House that night, and he will spend the September evening standing in the Rose Garden, with his top button undone and his tie loose, staring up at the cotton candy sky thinking about his dad.

PRIDE BEFORE THE FALL

"Dad... should we wait for Mom to hang the garland?"

"I can do it."

"But you have to use the ladder."

"I can do it."

Dylan and I stand in the shadow of the front door. I hold one end of a six-foot length of garland, and my son holds the other end. Cindy is out shopping on a post–Thanksgiving afternoon, and under the incessant urging of my only child who still believes with his little-beating-heart Santa Claus is real, I'm summoned to decorate the house for Christmas.

Even before my brain went bad, I never liked putting up Christmas decorations. Call me Scrooge, but the tedious effort has never filled me with spirit or merriment or jolliness. Chapped fingers and tangled cords of frustration do not appeal to me. Nor does the wire reindeer with uneven hooves, or the inflatable Santa who tips over like a fat drunkard. And then there's the blinking icicle lights that refuse to blink. Clark Griswold I am not.

But today it's unseasonably warm and, knowing this might be the last Christmas with the fleeting "Santa is real" magic, I submit. I slip on my sneakers, do the fatherly thing, and tell Dylan we can decorate. "Get the stepladder from the garage."

"But Mom can—"

"I can do it."

Throughout my teaching career, I lectured on the fragility of the male ego. So much of literature, both past and present, exposes the sad male reaction when his ego is stripped and shattered: *Macbeth. Death of a Salesman. One Flew over the Cuckoo's Nest. Fight Club.* If literature is a reflection of history, then the original sin of pride has doomed men, nations, and civilizations since Adam ate the apple. Julius Caesar. Napoleon. John Wayne. Donald Trump.

Men are hardwired to hide their inadequacies. We're not permitted to admit sickness or weakness or failure. When we lose or are publicly embarrassed, we often short-circuit. We set fire to cities. Send mean tweets. Refuse to listen to the logical decrees of a seven-year-old. Men don't know how to handle such impotence. We lie and yell and grow quiet and tell our kid to get the stepladder. In these most vulnerable moments, we get desperate. We take uncalculated risks, ignoring potential dangers to prove to whoever is watching that we're still men. To prove we're okay.

Endearing and honest, Rudyard Kipling offers a set of timeless "rules" for being a good person in one of my favorite poems, "If—". He writes:

If you can keep your head when all about you

Are losing theirs and blaming it on you

As Dylan drags the stepladder across the lawn, I roll my left shoulder like you do before you go bowling.

"Dad, we can wait for Mom."

"I'll be fine."

The day before Labor Day, I had fallen. Hard. I had attempted to lock the front door, but before I could reach the door handle, my brain hiccuped, and I lost my balance. I fell on my left shoulder. For a month, I suffered. I winced when I put on deodorant. Rolling on it while I slept woke me up. I wore hoodies and kept my left arm tucked in the front pouch like a sling. I hid the pain for weeks

188

until reaching for a napkin at dinner. The pain almost knocked me out of my chair. The orthopedic doctor explained my shoulder was not sitting correctly in the socket due to an impingement, and physical therapy would be the only way to improve it. I'm at week ten of physical therapy now. I'm feeling okay.

I open the stepladder, and Dylan's big blue eyes look up at me. What you're about to witness is the stupidity of the male ego. Right now, it's more than just garland. It's a primordial weakness. A DNA mutation. Counterfeit initiation into a bogus fraternity. Even if it's perilous to our health, we'll take our chances. Test our earthly limits. Bones heal, but bruised souls do not.

I should say, "Son, you're right. This is silly. I should wait for Mom. I should ask for help." But Adam ate the apple. Icarus flew too close to the sun. It's woven deep into our camouflaged mythology.

Son, you're so young. There's so much to learn. But with a hole in my brain and an impinged shoulder, I will ignore your suggestion and I will ascend this stepladder, toward the suburban sun. With my one good arm, I'll hang this most excellent garland for the glory of humankind.

"Dad, are you okay?"

My hands choke the sides of the ladder. I wobble my right foot up to the first step. Wobble up the left. Dylan is silent, and I'm sure, at some point, the word "sad" floats by his young eyes.

I'm six inches off the ground. My head spins. My heart thumps. *Deep breaths.* "I'm fine."

White-knuckled, I wobble my right foot up to the second step. Then the left. I'm on the top step. Twelve inches off the ground. Flying now. Alone. A man straddling the apex of his mountain. I'm sure the male impulse to ignore his shortcomings and the foolhardy belief he can emerge a champion—just this one time—is responsible for many home improvement mishaps.

Dylan hands up the garland, and with my one good arm, I slowly lace the garland across the door trim. The job takes little time. Coming down the ladder is much easier and faster for me. Such is life. Dylan and I step back, admire the garland, and look as if we both know what we're doing.

It's too soon to tell the damage done on this warm November day. Yes, we hung the garland. But at what cost? What did I just teach my son? Years from now, when Dylan is faced with risk, I fear he'll remember how I appeared poised and defiant and forged ahead on the stepladder. *If Dad, with his bad brain and bad shoulder, can hang a garland...*

I don't want to say this too loud, but I struggle greatly with how my health has emasculated me. I can't play sports with my kids. I can't walk a straight line. My voice now dips and weaves with slurs and stumbles. I want Dylan to know letting go of my previous life and accepting this new one has been hard. When my son becomes a man, he will be forced, like all men, to do the same. Let go and accept. It's not easy. It's manly work. To leave the frat house. To go on your own. To trust yourself. To redefine yourself. For the good of yourself. For the good of others.

But old habits die hard and sometimes, when the adults leave me home alone, I regress. Don't we all? I still have a restless spirit. Don't we all? And I try to get away with little things, like hanging garland, to polish my glass ego. To prove to Adam and Icarus and John Wayne and every other man in the history of men that I'm still part of their foolish fraternity.

"It looks good, Dad."

"It does. Now don't tell Mom."

THE FIRST DAY OF THE REST OF MY LIFE

I look at the clock: 6:54 a.m. The school bus will be at the corner in three minutes. I had spent seventeen years grinding through morning traffic as I scratched mental notes for first period. I was an object following Newton's first law of motion, not changing states because no force had made me do so. In late September of 2020—feeling the joint forces of a pandemic, my children growing up, and the hole in my brain further compromising my vision, speech, and balance—I changed my motion. I turned in my retirement paperwork and changed my direction.

When I told Haley, Chase, and Dylan I was taking time off from teaching to attend to my health and spend more time with them, they didn't have much to say. I turned to Haley, the oldest, the "spokeschild" of the litter. I said, "I'll now be here in the morning to get you off to school."

"Okay."

"Aren't you excited?"

"Sure."

At first, I was taken aback, annoyed at my kids' indifference. My own kids had just shrugged. Then I realized they're so young. Time is not an urgent matter. They can't imagine growing up and getting old. They can't imagine anything beyond today. To them, things and people will always just be. To them—time is infinite.

Unlike my kids, every adult I told about my retirement had a reaction: "Wow!" or "Good for you!" or "Best of luck!" A well-studied friend called leaving teaching, "an exercise in courage." A less-studied friend nodded and said, "Takes some balls."

I can't claim courage. I just know as you age you begin to feel, in your brittle bones, how frail and ephemeral life is. Children become adults. Parents die. Teachers retire. Diseases progress. Time becomes our most valuable yet often least appreciated resource. You face the most difficult of human questions, "How will I spend my time?"

That question had been asked and answered for me. Often I couldn't speak clearly, and teaching had grown too mentally taxing to continue. And so, on Friday, October 2, 2020, the same year that my father, the workingman, celebrated his planned retirement, I was forced to teach the last class of my career. Thanks to the pandemic, I had to do it virtually, from my living room.

For me, being a teacher was a job of last resort. If I couldn't make it as a journalist or a writer or a professional soccer player or a comedian or a rodeo clown, I would become an English teacher. I mean, how hard could teaching be? Most teachers I had in school either didn't care or made it look like they didn't care. Either way, I wouldn't have to work nights or weekends or summers. Teaching would, somehow, hand me the rare gift of infinite time. So, at twenty-two, with time on my side, I became a teacher.

I had seventeen years of novels and poems and essays. Of lecturing on characterization and themes and arguing why your fifth-grade English teacher was probably wrong about the rules of writing. Of standing in front of a classroom full of teenagers pretending I was comfortable being called a "teacher."

I'm proud of my work. I tried hard to make learning not only fun but relevant. I tried to be my most honest, vulnerable self. For the students' sake. For my sake. In fact, my best teaching work often happened in the privacy of my heart and mind. Standing in line at the food store or sitting in the waiting room at a dentist's office, I often

194

reflected on what it meant to be seventeen years old. To realize adulthood was near. To feel the squeeze of time. To doubt every decision they have or will have to make. To question courage. I would be lying if I told you I wouldn't miss those reflections.

Courage was the theme of the last class I taught. This was partly curriculum design, and partly me needing one last lesson on courage. After I told the students I was taking an extended break from teaching, after I thanked them, after I tried hard not to cry, I asked them to privately answer this question: When you read the word "courageous" who is the first person you think of?

I then read them the poem "Invictus" by William Ernest Henley, which concludes with the verse:

I am the captain of my fate

I am the master of my soul.

I told them I think every human being should read this poem every day, preferably before breakfast, until all verses are memorized and seared into the brain like Newton's first law of motion.

Then we read the chapter "Speaking of Courage" from Tim O'Brien's novel *The Things They Carried*, a story about a regretful soldier, Norman Bowker, who, after the Vietnam War, courageously returns home to Des Moines, Iowa. Bowker. Unsure what to do next with his life, he drives in a constant loop around a local park, replaying moments from before and during the war. If you've been with me for a while, you know my love for *The Things They Carried* and how fitting it was to read it on my last day.

Tim O'Brien and me in April 2019. Ocean County Community College, Toms River, New Jersey.

I had the students write an unedited letter to the person they first thought of when they read the word "courageous." Letter writing taught me more about writing than any English teacher I ever had. When you write a letter, you focus squarely on your audience. You attempt the hard work of human connection. And when you concentrate on your audience, your writing becomes emboldened and honest. Fierce and purposeful. You avoid onerous language and sophomoric drivel. Your words, if sharpened, cut bone. Like how T.S. Eliot, Toni Morrison, and Tim O'Brien have kept their words sharp even through the dullness of time. My writing advice is simple: Write letters. Yes, letter writing is therapeutic, reflective, and provokes the writer to choose their words carefully. But it also teaches a writer to emotionally invest in their writing. After many years of teaching English, I can confidently say, for most students, writing is not an emotional investment. Writing is a grade point average investment. A means to an end. An exercise in academic pretentiousness that on many nights left me bored and uncut.

But then, as quickly as my teaching career began, it all but ended. No brass bands. No cheerleaders. No confetti. No balloons. No white horse to ride into the sunset. No Board of Education members honking car horns outside my house. No Betsy DeVos standing on my porch with an Edible Arrangement.

Just the slow whirl of the ceiling fan above me, a cup of cold coffee in my hand, and the ache of a quiet house. As I shut down the virtual class on my computer and as the screen faded to black, it occurred to me that teaching and parenting and writing, and probably everything else in-between, are less about right and wrong and more about connection. Less about content and appearance and more about having the audacity to be yourself.

A few years before my last day, in the second week of school, a young man approached my desk after class and asked me if we could talk. I thought maybe it was to discuss his summer reading assignment grade or some of the novels I planned to teach in the upcoming school year. If you teach long enough, you develop an instinct to read students. In one glance, you can often tell the bookworms from the troublemakers. This kid, with his wire-rimmed glasses and black T-shirt tucked into his khaki pants, looked like a bookworm. Then the student said something like, "Um... this might be weird because we don't really know each other, but I wanted to talk to you about my father." We spent the next hour in a warm classroom, two strangers, talking and laughing and crying about our fathers.

In my final class, that very student appeared on the screen. His sister was in my class, and he was now a young man in grad school. He thanked me in front of the entire virtual class. He said he was sad I was leaving, and I was, even though we had not talked in years, still very important to him. He told me he's attending grad school, and I joked about feeling old. I joked about time being fleeting. I joked to hide the sadness in my throat.

The greatest joy of my career has been having an seventeen-year conversation with my students. Sure, the names and faces change, but the desire to connect did not. Connection, no matter how resistant we are to it, is how life is revealed to us.

I want to thank all of my students, both the living and the dead, for lending me their lives. For challenging me. For listening to me. For accepting my advice. For making my job, dare I say, fun. And please know, despite high school's final celebration jazzed up with "Pomp and Circumstance" and tassels and diplomas and a marching band and packed football stadiums on soft June evenings, the human story never graduates. It progresses from one stage of experience to the next. It has been and continues to be an honor, to be a character, for better or worse, in so many of their stories.

But as the protagonist of my own story, rather than making sure to be there for their first-period class, I'm still here at 6:54 a.m., leaning on the counter, sipping from a mug of hot coffee. I hear the sweet patter of my children's growing feet run from the bathroom to the bedroom. There's a rustle of a school bag. A zip of a lunch bag. The early morning swirls with youthful energy.

Somebody shouts, "What time is it?"

I clear my throat and say, "Time to go."

Being awarded "Teacher of the Year" in 2016.

Hosting the annual "Prom PowerPoint," which grew to mythical status at my high school. It was a 45-minute presentation on "how to prom." I taught the students the history behind prom, how to greet and compliment their date, how to pose for pictures, and how to dance. Some students took my class just for the "Prom PowerPoint."

2017 Graduation Commencement speech

A PEACEFUL TRANSFER OF POWER

The day before President Biden's inauguration, on January 19, 2021, I sit on the couch watching TV. A red pixelated banner with the white-lettered question "A PEACEFUL TRANSFER OF POWER?" hangs on the screen in the soft blue sky over the White House.

This past year I've taken more of an interest in politics than ever before, but I'm forty now. It's a requirement. Just like selecting more supportive sneakers, taking vitamins, browsing supermarket circular ads, and obsessing over the electric bill. (I'll bet your kids think electricity is free too.) But despite its title, this story is not political. I feel I don't have enough history, enough political intelligence, enough take-your-opinion-and-shove-it American tact to gracefully write about politics. So I won't. Also politics, for the most part, bores me.

My cell phone, keeping me company on this quiet Tuesday afternoon, vibrates on the couch next to me. It's the email I'd been waiting for. The subject line reads: "Resignation Letter." For almost half of my life, I've identified myself, for better or worse, as a teacher. This week, the same week America swears in a new President and transfers power, I take a step toward a permanent leave from teaching, attempting to transfer my power to a new identity.

I read the email. The past seventeen years sits heavy in my chest. I see my younger self standing on a student's desk reciting Hamlet's "To be or not to be" soliloquy. I see the bouquet of fake flowers that have been rooted to my desk for years. My silver coffee mug is there. So are the gray canvas Adidas sneakers I wore every day. I smell markers and chocolate chip cookies from the baking class down the hall. I see the Lightning McQueen lunch kit I started to take to school when one of my kids became too cool for character lunch kits. I'm seeing the scenery that defined my life for so many years in the nouns and verbs of this email. The scenery I took for granted. The scenery I already miss. I see yellow Post-its with blue-inked handwritten notes, a running list of poems I taught, a tattered copy of *The Catcher in the Rye,* and the Muhammad Ali poster I hung in my classroom every year. A stuffed Simba a student bought me sits by my computer. I see the first classroom I ever taught in: Room 201 with its glossy black and gray tile floor, old-school chalkboard, and rows of wooden desks. And the late afternoon sunlight slanting through the window warming my desk, strewn with student essays. And I sit there, young and clean-shaven, loosen my tie, exhale, and convince myself I will never survive my first year of teaching.

I look up from my phone.

The TV flashes scenes from January 6, 2021: a hunting party in the US Capitol. You've seen the images. The shaky camera. The smoke. A noose. Fists. Blood. White granite steps. The shattered windows. The rush of bodies, tissue and bone, resisting institutional change. I look down, read the email again, and the past and the present collide.

One of my favorite things to explain to my students was how, in literature, a character's internal landscape often mirrors their external landscape. For example, in *A Streetcar Named Desire*, the slums of New Orleans reflect the hardness of Stanley Kowalski. Or how Scotland's unraveling government rivals King Macbeth's internal unraveling. Or how the decay of Pride Rock mirrors the moral decay of Scar. This last one was from the animated film, *The Lion King*. Every year I would teach *The Lion King* around spring break when cartoons were the only thing that would keep students' attention.

Maybe I'm being trite or maybe I'm still trying to be a teacher or maybe I'm just trying too damned hard to write this, but we are living in a uniquely American moment. On my couch, in my sweatpants, history collides with my inbox, with my heart. What is happening out there among the stone pillars of Washington, DC, is happening here on the foam and microfiber of my couch.

America the brave is reluctant to transfer power and so am I. Like much of the literature I taught over the years, the turmoil of the outward landscape reflects a character's internal landscape. As I watch the rebellious acts of January 6, I feel closer to America than I've ever felt. Because we, the land and I, are wounded and trying to make sense of what just happened.

Everyone I know (and I do not know any politicians, dictators, or Real Housewives of Ocean County) is attempting a transfer of power. How many people do you know who are going through a change? Getting married. Having a baby. Starting a new job. Going back to school. Moving to a new city. Retiring.

America, right now, is teaching us that the quality of our life comes down to how we transfer our power. We saw what happens when that transfer is met with resistance. A rebellion. An insurrection. Every time I watch the news and see Congress attacked, I feel more scared, more hopeless, more uncertain about our future.

Maybe we can learn something from these chaotic January days. Maybe the reason why life is so complex is because we can't decide how to transfer our power. Do we resist? Or do we accept? I read the email again. My jaw tightens. My stomach flutters. And I choke back tears I felt coming on for months. America and I are attempting to transfer power. Both of us resisting. Both of us broken. Both of us, in the throes of our young histories, spectacularly short of what we might become.

GETTING BOOED

Today I'm watching Chase's baseball game under the kind of American sky baseball was invented for. Soft sunshine. A high blue sky. Tumbles of white clouds. It's the third inning. A pitch is thrown, a bat is swung, and a baseball careens toward me over the first base fence. Seated in one of those cheap, collapsible sideline chairs I extend both arms out in front of me.

The baseball floats over the high, chain-link fence. I shift my weight in my chair. Because old instincts die hard, I reach out my hands like a bowl and wait. The ball falls toward me. Gravity and fate intersect again. But this time, the ball bounces off my hands and tinkles across the soft, green grass.

An old man in a red Phillies cap boos me. It isn't a nasty, guttural boo. Not the kind of boo Philadelphia sports fans are notorious for. Not the kind of boo reserved for the New York Mets. No, it's a soft, almost sweet, lips-slightly-parted boo. The kind of boo you reserve for mild antagonists like under-cooked pizza or dead remote-control batteries.

History suggests the act of booing dates back to ancient Greek plays. If the play failed to entertain, the wine-guzzling audience would jeer at the actors' performance, the boos thundered into a loud, extended "BOOOOOO." The actors were ushered off stage, and the play was often never performed again. Though Philadelphia didn't invent the boo, the impulse to boo has been encoded into our regional DNA. When someone, or something, is not fulfilling its potential, we boo.

History also suggests Philadelphia's reputation for booing originated on October 5, 1931, at Game Two of the World Series between the St. Louis Cardinals and the A's, when President Herbert Hoover was introduced to a sold-out Shibe Park. According to Joe Williams, reporter for *The New World Telegram*, President Hoover was met with "… a vigorous, full-rounded melody of disparagement."

Aside from having the guts to introduce myself to Cindy, my second greatest adolescent achievement was catching a homerun ball during the 1996 MLB Homerun Derby at Philadelphia's Veterans Stadium. It was a muggy July afternoon when Brady Anderson, outfielder for the Baltimore Orioles, hit a towering homerun down the right field line toward me. I reached out, and by gravity and fate, the baseball fell into my glove. And why wouldn't it? I was young and naive and believed everything would always be within my reach.

Later that night, using a thing called a VCR, I recorded what I forever etched in my private mythology as "The Catch." For a brief moment, the TV camera held just long enough for the entire world to see me pull the ball from my glove and hold it in the air like a leather-bound sun.

The hardest thing for me to accept right now is that I can no longer physically do some things I once did. Forget riding a two-wheeled bike. Forget skiing. Forget diving in the ocean. Steps are a problem. Walking while holding a full glass of water is a problem. Catching a baseball is certainly a problem. Yes, I know, age diminishes abilities. But this is different. There's an unnatural disharmony, a failed connection; my brain speaks a language my body no longer understands. This often leaves me feeling frustrated, like a stranger in a strange land, and yearning for a time when my brain and body were in sync.

The old man in the Phillies hat lets out a soft, "Boooo."

Maybe I deserve the heckle. Maybe I don't. But being a Philadelphia native, I understand the "boo." It is an abbreviated way of saying, "C'mon, you can do better." And maybe I can. Maybe I can do a better job of letting go of the past and accepting what I can't control. Like gravity and fate. Like *cerebellar atrophy*. Like an old man's disapproval.

And so, on a perfect American evening, the uncaught baseball sits in a ray of sunlight like so many things now, just out of reach.

THE "GET UP": THE REMIX

In a soft little boy voice, Dylan asks me, "Dad, can we go outside and have a catch?"

I bend down and say, "Sure. Just let me put on my shoes." And then I fell. Sometimes my falls are spectacular. Windmills and waves. Jerks and jives. Shuffles and shakes. Like the unscripted gyrations of James Brown or Mick Jagger...

But this was not one of those times. No Jitterbug. No Twist. No Carlton. No Floss. No warning. Just down like a bag of suburban cement.

"Whoa. Dad, are you okay?"

"I'm fine."

In the last few months these unspectacular falls have been happening more often. In the spring of 2021, "The Get Up" was published in an anthology of short, nonfiction stories called *Dear 2020: Letters to a Year That Changed Everything*, edited by Chris Palmore. Everything I wrote then is still very much true, but I feel something else today. A residual effect of my youngest son witnessing his father's fall: shame.

Since the beginning of time, fathers have expressed their love for their children through instruction. In primitive times, it was decided men were not natural nurturers. We were hunters and protectors. Our family's survival was our chief duty. And this required us to be stoic, guarded, and protective. We could not be distracted by articulating our feelings. So we conditioned ourselves to avoid talking about important things inside. A father taught his children to track animals, to hunt, to farm, to build fires. Physical exertion forged an emotional connection. This father-showing-child-doing ritual expressed what fathers often struggled to say. It's how we promoted 200,000 years of masculinity.

In less primitive times, say the 1980s, my father showed his love by showing me how to play baseball, swing a hammer, and push a lawn mower. His instruction, his hands guiding my movements, was a form of wordless love. An urge to instruct our children in how to do things has been encoded in our DNA. It's primal. But how does a father show his love, when he can't physically show his children how to do things?

"Do you need help?"

"Sure."

Without instruction, Dylan moves a chair over to me. I lean on the seat, pull myself up, and get up. I can't speak for all men, but I struggle with not being able to do physical things with my kids. It feels unnatural just to watch them learn how to do things on their own. I once wrote that I thought I'd do physically heroic dad things, like carry all three children off to bed tucked under my arms like footballs or run 5k's together. But we age and learn that real life falls incredibly short of the one we imagined. And yet, despite our protests, it's the unplanned life that teaches more than our fantasies ever could.

Little did I know, seven years later, I would still be living an unplanned life. Still struggling to accept I will not do the physically heroic dad things I once dreamed of. Though my body is now indifferent to 200,000 years of heredity, I'm still tethered to a father's duty to instruct. My instruction looks different now. Like writing publicly about personal struggles. Like accepting help from others. Like getting up after you fall. Like making peace with your shame.

"Dad, maybe we can have a catch later."

Standing again, I look at him, and smile, "I would like that."

It's soul-crushing to not become the dad I thought I would be. The man I imagined I'd become. But here's the simple truth: Life is a remix. Life will always be different than we imagined. Unexpected things will happen. Things that will reshape our reality. But it's our responsibility, whether we like the beat or not, to put on our shoes and accept the remix. To alter our expectations, adapt, and even dance to the new, unfamiliar rhythm.

BEFORE I TURN OFF THE LIGHTS: LETTER #4

Dear Chase,

It's 2021 and you're ten. Based on your current detestation of reading, and given this letter is stitched in the middle of a book, you probably won't read this book or this letter soon, even if they are written by your dad.

Knowing this, I wrote this letter to the eighteen-year-old you, hoping you've developed a slight tolerance for reading by 2029. By then you'll, unofficially, be a man. Certainly, you'll feel the squeeze of adulthood. The pressure to assign yourself to a profession. I don't know what you'll dream of being in 2029. Maybe a gym teacher or a professional social media influencer. But now, in 2021, you dream of becoming a professional baseball player.

You've talked about playing shortstop in big-league

stadiums, maybe for the Phillies or the Angels, being on TV, and making millions of dollars. You've even promised me a good seat behind home plate with all-you-can-eat hotdogs. You've impressed your coaches with how well you've listened, how focused you were, and how you played baseball with a Labrador-playing-fetch joy in your heart. I want you to know that watching you stretch a single into a double on a perfect summer evening made your dad feel like a kid again.

But you're eighteen now and it's time you heard the hard truth: dreams don't always come true. Life, like baseball, gets increasingly difficult. A lot has to go right for you to turn pro. Your body must remain injury free. Your mind must remain level and humble. You must be wary of praise. You must keep your enthusiasm. Ability and fate and luck must synchronize their watches. And amid the distractions of adolescence, you must commit to the daily grind of improving your swing, your footwork, your fielding, your agility, your strength, and your hand-eye coordination.

I hope when you read this in 2029, my delusions of you having already been drafted and featured in Sports Illustrated have become true. And maybe you're reading this on a chartered flight to the Phillies spring training facility in Florida. Or maybe you're in a swanky New York City steakhouse, sitting on a red-leather couch, awaiting a shiny-shoed agent attempting to woo you and your .305 batting average.

But what if my delusions are just delusions? What if your baseball dream doesn't come true? What if, in 2029, you're simply a B+ high school kid trying on tuxedos for prom? What if you just received another college rejection letter? What if you stock shelves at the local supermarket and play slow-pitch softball on Sundays? If this happens, promise me before you graduate from high school, you'll have the courage to dream a new dream.

The ugly side of adulthood is that after an adult realizes their childhood dream will not happen, they sometimes cannot dream a new dream. Donuts, sports gambling, tax evasion, and oxycodone will always have an adult audience. Failing to dream a new dream is deadly. It's a surefire way to get lost in a life that you do not want. Maybe your new dream will not have the pinstripe romance of a big-league ballplayer. So what?

There is a real cost to not chasing your dream, no matter how unromantic, how ordinary, the new dream may seem. Whether it's hitting a baseball or selling insurance or hanging drywall, you must chase a dream that fulfills the deeper parts of yourself. You must have the courage to do what's in your heart, in that hidden place where hope and joy wait—like prom dates—for the music to play, for the dancing to begin.

I also wanted to be a baseball player when I was ten. And then, at fourteen, I was cut from my high school baseball team. I spent years wondering what I should do next. In college, at twenty or twenty-one, I dreamed of becoming a writer who sold millions of books worldwide. And then, when I realized writing was hard work and most writers are lucky if they even sell a few dozen books, let alone millions, I became a high school teacher. But while I busied myself with teaching, the writing dream, like a stubborn update notification on your iPhone, remained. It wasn't until I got sick, turned forty, and retired from teaching that I accepted that notification. Maybe it was facing my mortality or the sudden gray stubble on my chin, but I realized we have little time to chase our dreams. And it makes little sense not to spend your life chasing your dreams.

I want you to know, if the baseball dream doesn't work out, it's okay. Many dreams do not come true. I will not love you any less. Even though it would be nice to watch a game behind home plate and stuff my face with hot dogs.

Listen, figure out your dream, not my dream or your partner's dream or whatever dream is trending on social media, and chase it with your Labrador heart. If you chase anything in this life, chase the dream that brings you joy. Live up to your name and chase the dream that can make possibilities become realities. Chase the dream with dogged persistence and boundless energy. One that makes your heart thump and flutter. Chase the dream that keeps you awake at night. Chase the dream you can share with others. The dream you may one day tell your children about. Chase the authentic dream. The worthy dream. The hard dream. The dream that will paralyze you with doubt and fear. Chase the dream that will soothe your soul. Chase the dream that will inspire others to chase their own dream. However, if your dreams are dashed, promise me, son, you'll have the courage to dream again.

Good night.

I love you.

See you in the morning.

PART IV: I'M NOT SLEEPING; I'M JUST RESTING MY EYES

GOOD ADVICE NEVER DIES

When I was a kid, my grandfather Mike "Pop" Stanton told me, "If you find yourself in a hole, stop digging.

I'm watching the 2020 post–election news coverage explaining that President Trump plans to file lawsuits against several states regarding alleged voter fraud. The TV talking heads seethe and shout and grow flush with frustration. They disagree with President Trump's unwillingness to concede the election.

"The President should accept the truth!" one person shouts.

"This is not truth. This is a lie," another retorts.

They begin shouting at each other. And at me. Not only is my dead grandfather talking to me but so is the TV. Everybody, these days, seems to have an opinion about what the President should do. What America should do. What you should do.

By all accounts, President Trump plans to roll up his starched sleeves, hand the lawyers shovels, and tell them to dig. And we, from the comfort of our star-spangled couches, have the luxury of watching.

Some thirty odd years ago, when I was around ten, I trailed behind my grandfather as he weed whacked around his red brick house on a hot summer day. Like a careless child, I accidentally kept stepping on the orange extension cord. With mighty tugs, my grandfather would pull the cord from under my feet and continue weed whacking until my lack of self-awareness annoyed him so much that he turned it off, led me by the hand to the garden, gave me a shovel, and instructed me to dig a hole.

"And then what?" I asked.

"Well, once you find yourself in the hole, stop digging."

So I dug and dug and dug as my grandfather and the weed whacker zipped around the yard. When he returned to the garden, I stood in the hole I had dug holding the shovel upright like a sword. Like a dirty tool of the highest honor.

"Why did you stop digging?"

"You told me if I found myself in a hole to stop digging."

"Good," he nodded. "Now get out of the hole."

While writing this book, I discovered my grandfather's advice was an old adage attributed to legendary American humorist, Will Rogers. He coined the phrase, "If you find yourself in a hole, stop digging."

I also discovered we're all addicted to digging holes. Digging a hole is a pointless endeavor unless we're digging for a purpose—planting a tree, burying a body, hiding a treasure. This year—2020—has been a year of digging holes. Our American muscles are tense. We are out of breath, blistered, and have calluses on our democratic hands. The election fallout, the lingering pandemic, smoldering racial tensions, financial straits. As the year comes to a merciful close, we're a nation looking up, searching for a way out.

But what about the holes in your personal life? Health holes. Relationship holes. Financial holes. Professional holes. We all have them. We're all in some untenable situation we're desperate to escape. There are unlimited ways to dig a hole. Cheating, lying, ignoring, hiding, shaming, and overindulging are all good shovels. We dig holes when we fail to accept the truth. We try to dig our way out of selfishness. But we do so without thinking. And mindless shoveling results in a tired mind, body, and spirit.

A few years ago, Dr. Reardon recommended I read the classic *Full Catastrophe Living* by Jon Kabat-Zinn. Kabat-Zinn explains how the practice of mindfulness can help alleviate symptoms of chronic illnesses and ultimately ease suffering. He also explains the dangers of "living on the treadmill of modern life." Meaning we're conditioned to always "do." We often are not mindful of our thoughts and actions. Why am I thinking this? Why am I doing that? And what is my reason for digging this hole?

This unconscious life on a treadmill instigates negative emotions—anger, confusion, sadness, unhappiness. Let's call them the "seeds of bad habits." It takes awareness and discipline to understand the fruits of your actions. To know you're digging a hole. To drop the shovel, before the calluses form, before the hole is too deep to escape. We must realize that the arbitrary act of digging a hole is a foolish waste of energy. A simple distraction for a kid exiled to a garden while his grandfather worked.

So the next time you dig—I hope you dig purposefully.

BOWLING WITH GOD

Chase and I are in the car together, and I'm driving. He's seven-years-old, tucked in the backseat, and it's raining. Of course, it's raining. Stories like this are almost always punctuated by weather.

With the windshield wipers on full tilt, a rumble of thunder rolls overhead and a flash of lightning splits the night sky in half. "Dad," Chase says, "did you know when there's thunder and lightning God is bowling in heaven?"

"Yeah bud, I did know that."

"How did you know, Dad?"

"Well, I went to Catholic school just like you, buddy. And my teachers told me the same thing."

Call it telepathy, call it being a parent, but I felt the questions forming like thunderclouds in his head. He's pondering the angles of time. He's attempting to comprehend the news that I was once a kid like him, unsure and curious, sporting a Catholic school uniform, and sitting quietly with folded hands as the teacher educated us on things like God and heaven and bowling.

The car eases to a traffic light and stops. The rain falls hard and heavy. The windshield fogs at its edges. "Dad, do you know who the Ultimate Warrior is?"

"The wrestler?"

"Yeah."

"Yes, I know who he is. Why?"

"Because he died."

"I know."

"Dad, he had cancer and he died."

"Hey, buddy, how did you know that?"

"YouTube."

The first person I ever really knew who died was my grandmother. I was sixteen when it happened. I remember not thinking much about her death. In a way, I guess, it made sense. She was old and sick, and she died. And that was that.

I catch Chase in the rearview mirror. His knees are pressed against his chest, feet up on the seat, and his oversized eyes watch the watery glow of streetlights and store signs flicker by. I'm envious. His little life is unbounded by theories of time, of the unnerving truth that I will one day die and won't be here to answer his questions.

The light turns green and we go.

The second person I knew who died was a close family friend, Joey. One night, for reasons still unknown, he hung himself with his karate belt in the bathroom. He was twelve. I was eighteen. He was happy and popular and had blond hair, but then he was dead.

I remember my dad, with wet eyes and strained words, explaining what happened, clearing his throat, working out the details. I remember saying I was fine. I remember going to school. I remember sitting in history class, staring out the window watching the morning bloom into its becoming and imagining what it must be like to be dead. Was it like my grade school teachers said? Was it peaceful and warm? Was everything highlighted in gold? Was God even there? If so, would he greet me? Would we go bowling? Would I have to bring my own shoes or does heaven have a shoe rental counter?

We cruise past the plastic heavens of suburbia—Target, Starbucks, Chick-fil-A. I was curious. I wanted to press the conversation. I wanted to know what my child knew about life, about death.

"Hey, Chase, do you know what happens when you die?"

"What?"

"Well, bud... you go to heaven."

"Oh yeah. They said that at school."

"So, Dad, is the Ultimate Warrior in heaven?"

"I think so."

"But he doesn't have cancer in heaven. Because you can't have cancer in heaven, right, Dad?"

"Chase, do you know what cancer is?"

"It means you're really sick."

"Kind of."

"Dad, do you have cancer?"

"No."

"Dad, when you die are you going to go to heaven?"

"Well, I hope so, bud."

"Because when you're in heaven, you're not sick anymore, and I know sometimes you're sick. That's what Mom says. So if you go to heaven, you'll feel better, right, Dad?"

"I hope so, bud."

"But if you're in heaven then you can't take me to my soccer games."

We merge onto the highway, race under an overpass, and things get quiet. The rain stops, and I digest the absoluteness of my son's declaration. I breathe and feel the spinning wheels and the pulsing engine, and the car charges toward the waiting darkness. There's an explosion of thunder, a flash of lighting, and just before we exit the quiet of the overpass, Chase calmly says, "But Dad, if you're in heaven you can meet the Ultimate Warrior. And then you and the Ultimate Warrior could go bowling with God."

Beyond the brim of the overpass, there looms thunder and lightning. I want to tell him I don't want to die. I want to tell him I love him, his siblings, and his mom. I want to tell him I'm scared I'll die before I have a chance to say what I need to say.

I squeeze the steering wheel, stiffen my wrists, catch Chase in the mirror again, and lacking something inside—maybe the courage to challenge his young beliefs, I lean my head back, brace myself for what's to come, and simply reply, "I hope so, buddy."

I hope so.

ADVICE FROM THE DEAD

Recently, while rummaging through stacks of dusty boxes to clean out the garage, I see a brown, unmarked envelope. Intrigued, I quit rummaging. I open the envelope and find my grandfather smiling on the inside. In the photo, it's 1954, and Pop was still years away from being Pop.

Mike "Pop" Stanton holding a pilsner glass. To his left stands his Uncle Al.

In this picture, he's just Mike. He's twenty-five-years old, and he just bought a bar on the corner of Cedar and Pacific Avenue in Wildwood, New Jersey. He renamed the place "Mike and Ed's," and he's serving drinks to a row of rowdy Philadelphians who had escaped the tightness of their row-home lives for the weekend promise of some New Jersey shore magic. It's early evening, and the bar is filled with thick, masculine laughter, which overpowers the bouncy doo-wop rhythm of "Life Could Be a Dream" flowing out of the jukebox. It smells of a different time. Of Old Spice and cigarettes.

I imagine moving across the checkered floor to an open seat at the end of the bar and watch Pop make small talk with a few friends with sunburned necks. He laughs, and it's hearty and deep, just like I remember. Pop looks up and nods as if he's been expecting me. He turns to the tap, pours a beer in a short pilsner glass, and brings it my way. His skinniness surprises me. But the eyes, the smile, the roundness of his shoulders are all there like they've always been.

Pop puts the glass down in front of me. His blue eyes meet my blue eyes, he lays his hand on top of my hand, and tells me how he appreciated the funeral, how he enjoyed the eulogy I delivered even though it was a bit brief. An entire life in 1,337 words? He thought I should've stretched it to at least 1,700.

He winks. Then his face gets serious. He tells me he's disappointed we paid full price for the luncheon after the funeral. He tells me he knows an Italian who rents a room behind the scrap yard along the Delaware River. He tells me the Italian would've catered the whole thing, funeral and luncheon, for half the cost.

He tells me he doesn't have long because other people need him. He tells me that death is a lot like life in that sense. Someone always needs you. Someone is always failing to listen. But death, he says, brings infinite patience. Sadly, life does not.

A drunk wearing a tilted fedora calls out, "Mike, Mikey boy, bring me over another one. I told the old lady I'd be home by seven and it's quarter of!"

Pop shoots the old man a wait-your-damn-turn-old-man look. A look he perfects when, in a few years, he becomes a police officer and spends late hours working the fanged streets of southwest Philadelphia.

He returns to me, "See what I mean, no patience." Then he gets serious again. Hard lines form around his eyes. "You know what the living say about the dead? About how, at least, the dead are in a better place?"

I nod.

"They're wrong! What the living fail to realize is that even though your setting changes, you do not. When you die you take yourself, for better or worse, with you to the other side. Look around. All these men came here thinking things would somehow be better. But they're miserable laying bricks in Philly and they're miserable drinking beer in Jersey. Fools. They thought by crossing the river, by changing states, their life would magically improve. Life. Death. They don't work that way."

He tightens his grip on my hand and says, "It's not where you are, it's who you are that matters. The same holds true for the afterlife. And you're going to mess a lot of things up. But if you can let love lead your way, you might do just enough to get it right. And if you can understand this while you're alive, I promise when your time comes, you'll cross that bridge a happy man."

He loosens his grip, drums his fingers on the bar, and looks out the window. His brow bent like mine when I'm contemplating something big. I study his profile the way I did when I was a kid tucked in the front seat of his white pickup truck.

I remember how he would be driving and singing with Frank Sinatra, and his profile would be glowing against the shifting sunlight.

When the chorus hit, he flashed a hard-earned smile, the smile of a man who made peace with his life, with the world. A smile I can't quite forget.

When his eyes return to mine, he tells me the beer was on the house. But that was it. No more freebies. This isn't a soup kitchen. And if I wanted another, I would have to pay for it or wash dishes.

Pop takes his hand from mine. He steps back, smiles like someone about to board a plane, and somehow defying the laws of earthly physics, I still feel the pressure of his hand resting on mine as he drifts away, down the length of the bar, tending to the others who need him.

A bead of sweat rolls down the glass. Heavy, hollow laughter steamrolls across the bar. Something sits in my throat. I want to call him back. I want to breathe with him again. I want to tell him I write stories about him so he doesn't seem so dead. I want to tell him how I miss him just a little more around Christmas. How I wish he could hold my children. How I wish they could experience his smile and hear his advice and feel the gentle pressure of his hand against theirs.

But I don't.

Because you can't. Because you can't tell the dead what they already know. Because when you open an envelope and you're greeted by the dead and they squint and speak, all you can do is listen, consider your mortal ways, and do your best to heed their eternal advice.

MY WORST DAY AS A TEACHER

Three years before I retired, on a Monday night in May, a student in my Advanced Placement Literature class died. In first period the next morning, I informed my class of twelfth graders that one of their classmates had died. The expressions on their faces made it clear they were hearing the news for the first time.

It was my hardest moment as a teacher. The classroom was silent. Then a girl in the back row by the window started to cry. And then another girl. And another. I tried to swallow down my sadness. But like so many times before, I cracked and cried. When the male students noticed, they began to cry too. Everyone in room A205 was crying.

When I had heard the news the night before, I was in shock. I was also at home and semi-removed from school. Cloistered in the comforts of my own self-indulgent world. But on a rainy Tuesday morning, with a classroom full of hopeful twelfth graders staring at me, it became painfully real. In your teenage years, you learn life is confusing, painful, and unfair. Bad things happen, often with little explanation.

I stood from behind my desk, walked across the front of the classroom, and threw out a balled-up tissue in the trash can. When I turned, Owen, biggest boy in the class, stood in front of me. I stared up at him. I could feel the wet eyes of the other students on us. Owen then put his thick arms around me and fell into me. I stumbled until my back hit the cinderblock wall. Owen, and all his dead weight, sobbed in my arms. He told me he had often given the kid who had died a ride to school. They would go to Taco Bell together, eat tacos, and talk politics. Then Owen, after a long sad silence, apologized for staining my polo shirt with tears and snot.

When I was a classroom teacher, I often expressed my own struggles and why I found writing to be a healing act. Sure, I was promoting academic growth too but, in such hard moments, I realized standardized tests and high GPAs and college acceptances mattered very little. Look, you and I don't know how long we have to live, and if you're like me, you've wasted a lot of life wanting and chasing frivolous things. Spent too much time trying to impress the wrong people or caring what the wrong people think.

Too much time procrastinating or being apathetic or ignorant.

Too much time complaining.

Too much time worrying about something that hasn't happened.

Too much time making excuses.

Too much time being timid.

Too much time being afraid.

Too much time being disillusioned.

Too much time ignoring the truth.

Death is our greatest teacher. He has never taken a sick day. Or a personal day. He is punctual and arrives to class with detailed lesson plans in his briefcase, takes attendance, clears his throat, stands at the front, and tells the truth: Life is short. You have less time than you think. If you don't take responsibility for your own life, you'll spend your precious time blaming others or blaming circumstances for your unhappiness. But you and I both know how easy it's to ignore the teacher. It's easy to gaze out the classroom window and wish we were somewhere else. It's easy to look around and ask, "Why should I care if no one else does?"

But recognizing the truths that death is teaching is an important step in learning how to use pain and suffering as a means toward growth. And no matter how excellent the teacher, students cannot and will not learn the material until they make a conscious choice to take responsibility for their own learning.

All I can hope is that you and I become good students and make that choice.

CELEBRATING VICTORY WITH THE DEAD

On Super Bowl morning, I head to Forest Hills Cemetery wearing my Eagles jersey. It's February in Philadelphia, and it's cold and raining. Chase stands by my side as we look down at the stone marking the birth and death of my grandparents, Mike and Doreen Stanton.

My grandparents grave on February 4, 2018. The day of Super Bowl LII.

I talk to them. I tell them about how the Eagles are playing in the Super Bowl tonight. How they're underdogs and have been underdogs throughout the playoffs. A real Philadelphia story.

Never having performed the earthly art of speaking to the dead, Chase stares up at me and then quietly drifts toward the car. I tell my grandparents I'm a bundle of emotions. Excited, nervous, with a hint of dread. I tell them I think we're finally going to win. I tell them I'll be thinking about them tonight. Chase's nose is pressed up against the car window. I'm sure his seven-year-old mind is convincing itself that Dad is a little stranger, a little more mysterious, than he previously thought.

An hour earlier, before the rain began, I had stared out my kitchen window into the calm, gray morning and listened to sports talk radio. Mary from Doylestown said she was going to wear her brother's Eagles jersey tonight. She said her brother taught her the Eagles fight song. How after high school he enlisted in the Army. And how on his first tour of duty in Afghanistan was killed by a suicide bomber.

Bill from Broomall said he'll be watching tonight's game from his recliner with his father's urn propped beside him. Like he's done all season.

Then two things happened before Jim from Norristown could finish his story about going to his first Eagles game at Franklin Field in 1960 with his parents who are now both deceased: One, I was on the verge of tears. Serious man-tears. And two, I had a sudden urge to visit my grandparents.

My grandparents were casual sports fans. They celebrated when Philadelphia celebrated. My grandfather was a Philadelphia police officer who told me stories about working security during Eagles games down on the Veterans Stadium field. How after the game he would visit the locker room and talk to the players. Which, when you're a kid, is just about the coolest thing in the world—much cooler than talking to wet cemetery grass.

Beyond that, I don't remember any conversations with either of them about sports. But that's not the point. My grandparents were fans of life. Fans of their children and grandchildren. They taught me the importance of togetherness, community, celebrations, and traditions. And since sports is a freeway that connects people, on Super Bowl Sunday, I wanted my grandparents to feel a part of the biggest game in Philadelphia sports history. To feel a part of the living story again.

Later, I watch the Eagles defeat the Patriots, 41 to 33, and capture the first Super Bowl title in franchise history. A franchise founded in 1933. When the clock settles on 0:00, I hug my mom and dad. I hug my brothers. I hug my wife and children.

After the celebration ends, I think about my grandparents. I'm sure Mary, Bill, and Jim are all hugging the spirits of their loved ones late into the night as well.

As children, our parents told us not to stress over striking out or missing a shot. They told us not to take it so hard. They told us that it's just a game. And now, as parents, we pass down the same sentiments to our children.

Don't take it so hard. Let it go. It's just a game. But I know it's not just a game. And my son now knows it's not just a game. Because hours before the Super Bowl, he listened to me talk to the dead. Because inside the earthly boundaries of the game, rests something ethereal that connects the living to the dead. A magical spell of muscle and bone that coaxes the dead to sit up and smile and celebrate the joy of sports, the joy of life with us once again.

Celebrating the Super Bowl LII victory with my brothers Keith (middle) and Kyle (right) and Chase and Haley. Dylan is offstage sleeping.

PS. Haley, Chase, and Dylan, if you become a Dallas Cowboys fan, don't call me.

WRITING TO RAISE THE DEAD

Early Saturday morning, I receive an email at 2 a.m. from a former student. She's leaving for Colorado State University in a few hours and can't find her Creative Writing final, a forty-page collection of poetry and personal essays she had written for my class. She writes, "I'm hoping you still have my project. If you do, could you send it to me? I wrote my heart out. I shared parts of my heart I had hidden from others." She had written about love, friendship, leaving her hometown, and about her classmate who died five days before the senior prom. She thanks me for teaching her about writing and about life. She says, "Like a toothbrush or pillow, I'm bringing your lessons with me."

Then she says she misses writing.

I close her email, find her final project in my files, and send it to her. A few hours later, she thanks me with a lot of exclamation points and wishes me luck with the upcoming school year. I've taught writing for nineteen years. By my own assessment, I've only taught writing well for the last nine. For the first ten years, I didn't know what I was doing. I taught writing the way you read instructions for assembling cheap furniture. Dispassionate. Indifferent. Rushed.

I respect and understand that, for some of us, writing is just something you have to do. A requirement. A chore. A nuisance. Even a waste of time. But for others, writing is as essential as a pillow or a toothbrush. Writing comforts when you're far from home or when a friend dies. Writing offers peace and perspective and reminds you that you're fully alive. And writing, real writing, takes guts and thought and imagination as if you're responsible not only for decorating the living room but also for inventing the furniture.

In August 2019, a friend with cancer died. She had one of those big laughs that came from somewhere deep inside her lungs—a laugh I secretly wished I had. Hours before I learned of her death, I had stepped onto my porch to toss chicken on the grill for dinner. It had been bright and sunny and raining. A summer sun shower. I had stood watching the rain fall and, as it so often does, memory had taken over and I lost my attachment to the present world.

It's now January, and I'm leaning against a granite kitchen counter I'm once again lost in memory. My friend with cancer stands before me. Shaved head, paper-thin skin, and electric eyes that dance like a pair of candle flames. My children are there, behind her, sitting at the kitchen table, staring at me as I try not to cry. I can sense the real world around me. The heat from the grill. The rain falling on leaves. But I'm not on the porch. I'm in the kitchen.

As if looking through an empty beer bottle, the kitchen is amber and blurry at its edges, but my friend with cancer is clear standing there before me. She is close and earnest and cups my cheeks with her hands. Looking into my eyes, she says, "I fucking love you."

I cry. My children watch. They don't ask questions. They just know things are serious when Dad cries.

I hug my friend. I can feel her bones shift under her skin. I feel her lungs work hard for air. She's in my arms and she's alive. Fiercely and forever alive. We let go of each other and say goodbye. That was the last time I ever held my friend.

My friend was special. An energetic and fiery woman who loved people. Never shy. Never afraid to laugh. She bottled joy and was eager to share with anyone sitting at the table. She was a master of ceremonies, loved her martinis, and was always game for a good time. She grew up with my mom and became my adopted aunt. She took me to concerts and baseball games. She had a husband, a son, and a dog, and it was difficult to tell which one she loved most. A free spirit, she once hitchhiked from Pennsylvania to California. She told me how she loved being on the open road. Driving into the unknown with the windows down and the radio on. Freedom. Possibility. Aliveness.

Doctors had given her four months. She lived for fifteen months. Even in her final weeks, when breathing and eating were hard, she still roared with laughter. She laughed as if she would never die. And maybe she didn't. Maybe her body simply couldn't hold her spirit any longer.

She was, and still is, all heart.

Windows down just driving into the unknown.

School doesn't teach you that writing is a form of magic. But it is. See, I'm writing these words because I want my friend to be alive again. By telling you about her, she's suddenly breathing on the page. She's cupping your cheeks. You can feel her bony fingers against your face. She calls you "doll" and is looking at you as if you're the most important person in the room. Because when my friend talked to you, you were. Writing allows you to bring back the dead. Something public education frowns upon. Something I don't. Maybe it helped my student resurrect her classmate.

In our final conversation, my friend had encouraged me to keep writing. "Keep writing stories. People need stories," she said. And this is why I write every day. Because my friend is dead and she told me to keep writing, and by writing I can make her talk again. Make her sip a Lemon Drop martini again. Make her laugh until she loses her breath again. I can make my dead friend hug me when I miss her, when tears fill my eyes. Like right now.

OLD MAN AND THE TEE

Cindy's grandfather passed away this week. Like many people born before the Great Depression, he was simple and honest. A "salt of the earth" type. A clean-your-tools-when-you're-done-working kind of man. A gardener. A woodworker. He put so much of himself into everything he brought to life: cucumbers and tomatoes, roses and evergreens, nightstands and bookshelves. His callused hands birthed so many things into the world that, without him, I fear the world will forever fall short of what it once was or will ever be again.

He hosted Thanksgiving dinners. His lawn, always green and trim, was the envy of his neighborhood. For years, he decked his house with so many Christmas lights and ornaments that he was featured in the local papers. He did it all with an effortless joy that I suspect anyone who ever met him secretly envied. On our wedding night, after a few Crown Royals, he put his arm around me, pulled me close, pointed to Cindy, and said, "If you're good enough for my granddaughter, you're good enough for me."

I had this story pinned to my "stories-to-write" list for a while. But writing, like life, is easy to procrastinate. Until the phone rings. Until your wife breathes "No" through tears. Until you just sit, in a quiet house, and listen to her cry. Until you feel empty. Until you regret the things you never said. Until you replay stories about a good man in your head and you cry because you know, with bone certainty, the story you're telling yourself is now a eulogy.

It's the summer of 2006, and I'm twenty-six. Strong, spry, and still resembling my college-soccer-playing days. Pop-Pop was seventy-nine. He had doorknobs for knees, a degenerative hip, and was legally blind in his right eye. Yet he had still golfed five days a week with that effortless joy. Around the clubhouse, he was a celebrity. The grounds crew, the other golfers, and the kid in the Cubs hat behind the concession counter knew him by name, George. He had his own golf cart and his own key to it. Our morning coffee was always on the house, yet he insisted on paying. It was what I imagine golfing with Arnold Palmer was like.

My golf game is wildly inconsistent. According to Pop-Pop, I try too hard. I still have the youthful propensity to complicate what is a relatively easy game. "Just hit the ball in the hole," Pop-Pop would shout as I whiffed and thrashed on the fairway turf.

Pop-Pop's ball somehow always stayed on the fairway. I'd hit one shot fit for the PGA tour, but then the next would slice deep into the rough. What his shots lacked in speed and distance, he made up for with killer accuracy. His strokes were smooth and effortless, and it seemed like even his golf ball was enjoying itself on a warm summer morning.

My biggest problem on the golf course is driving. I want to pound the golf ball into submission. I want my back swing to split the world in half. I want the romance of a three-hundred-yard drive. I want to impress Arnold Palmer with my drive (if he ever wandered onto the course).

At each hole, I would stride to the tee box with my driver in hand. I would push my tee into the soft turf and top it with my neon green ball. Taking a deep breath, I'd straddle the ball with my feet shoulder width apart, fantasize about sending the ball like some neon green comet into the blue morning sky, and then, in the quiet moment before I swung, Pop-Pop would softly say, "You keep your eye on the tee, and I'll watch your ball."

Whack. "Shit." He'd exclaim.

With my eyes locked on the uprooted tee, I would ask, "What?"

"I lost your ball."

Of course he did. He's seventy-nine. And has just one good eye.

Before every hole over the summer, Pop-Pop had promised to track my ball after every drive and after every drive he would lose my ball. Every hole. Every drive.

After a round of golf, we would sit in the shade of his front porch and look out over his well-kept lawn. He would have a tall glass of iced Crown Royal in his hand while I held a can of beer. I would fall into the warmth of his stories about growing up on a farm in Trenton, about climbing up to the crow's nest of his Merchant Marine ship to shoot gliding seagulls, and about how there would be traffic jams on his street when he finished decorating his house for Christmas.

And then after a long, comfortable silence, he would say something like, "You know, golf is not about strength. It's about patience."

Then I would say something like, "Yeah, but how do you make it look so easy?"

And he'd reply, "I guess I learned not to try so hard."

Peace be with you, Pop-Pop. May your effortless joy fly like a well-struck Titleist straight to my heart.

BEFORE I TURN OUT THE LIGHTS: LETTER #5

Dear Dylan,

Please read this letter thirty minutes after you become a dad.

Congratulations my son, you're a dad! Life as you know it is over. Now is a good time to remind you that when you were seven years old and were asked, "What do you want to be when you grow up?" you responded, "a dad."

Though your dream melted many hearts, it terrified mine. I had to figure out the complex, near impossible, and ancient problem of how to be a good dad. A problem you're tasked with right now. So let me be the first to welcome you to the confusing, sticky, land of children. Where your sleep, dietary habits, aspirations, sanity, and fantasy football championships are now merely footnotes in this new chapter in your life.

Writing about being a dad makes me uncomfortable. Even with years of experience, I feel inadequate giving fatherly advice in the same way I feel inadequate giving advice about the stock market, Russian doll collections, cosmetic dentistry, or ice fishing. However, I have found refuge in the following truth: Every dad is learning on the job. And when you learn on the job, you make mistakes. Maybe that's what makes a good dad. A man who is honest and reflective enough to learn from his mistakes.

I know a father's advice carries weight. As I sought advice from my dad about being a dad, you may do the same to me. Of course, you have the right to disagree with my advice. And as my child, I almost expect you to. However, I'm not sharing my advice with you for agreement. I'm hoping my advice will help you ease the burden of the demanding career you sought when you were a starry-eyed seven-year-old child.

Here are seven ways to be a good dad:

1. Accept that you're not always right.

2. Eat dinner with your family every night.

3. Set clear rules and expectations for your children to follow

4. Tell your children you're proud of them. (They should already know how much you love them.)

5. Learn how to do all the chores in the house so you can show your children how to correctly do all the chores in the house.

6. Value reading, exercise, and honesty.

7. Laugh with your children every day.

PS. Should something change and you don't become a dad, please continue to follow #1 and #6. And please know, I'm forever proud of you.

PPS: Goodnight.

I love you.

See you in the morning.

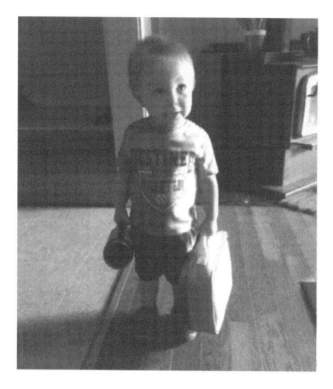

Dad-in-training. 2015.

PART V: A MAN CANNOT BE A FATHER WITHOUT LOVE

FIFTEEN YEARS OF IMPROV (AND MARRIAGE)

A gaggle of teachers stands nervously in a loose circle in the middle of a classroom. Before the students come back, teachers often have to endure "professional development" led by a training organization of the administration's choosing. There are a few laughs, awkward silences, and a lot of sweaty palms. I feel exceedingly uncomfortable too.

The instructor, Ms. Katie, tells us, "Improvisational exercises are a great way to get to know your coworkers. To ease the tension of a new school year." No one smiles. The instructor goes on to explain the "rules" of improv. Ms. Katie smiles, puts her hands on her hips and says,

"Make clear statements. Be open to the scene's possibilities. There are no mistakes. Listen to your partner—"

Someone checks their watch.

"Any volunteers?"

No one volunteers.

Ms. Katie, a bubbly brown-haired woman in a polka dot sundress from New York City, tells us one of the golden rules of improv is letting your partner finish their sentence. "Cutting them off—, topping them in conversation is an improv disaster. Listening to your fellow improviser is a quiet way to say, 'you're appreciated.'"

Today is June 24, 2020. Tomorrow, Cindy and I will celebrate our fifteenth wedding anniversary. Thinking about it, the rules of improv might also be the rules of marriage:

Make clear statements.

Be open to the scene's possibilities.

There are no mistakes.

Listen to your partner.

After fifteen years of marriage, my one takeaway would be that marriage is the ultimate improv game. Improv is challenging and embarrassing. It makes you uncomfortable, forces you to make snap decisions. It reminds you, rather awkwardly, you're doing something for the first time, and mistakes will be made.

There is no script. No director in a polka dot sundress feeding you lines. You must listen to your partner, respond to their dialogue and gestures, and be open to the scene's possibilities. Marriage, much like improv, is an experiment. On stage or in the living room, things will not go as planned. Marriage is hard and people are complicated. We do an outstanding job of hiding our vulnerabilities— fear, loneliness, and shame. And yet, we're not good at revealing parts of ourselves we don't fully understand or are embarrassed by.

Cindy and I on a rare date without kids.

For Cindy and me, after fifteen years of improv, our most demanding exercise was the scene of my diagnosis—the one where they told us my cerebellum is slowly degenerating. If anything, as a couple, we've learned to improvise, albeit unwillingly, when to laugh, when to cry, when to be honest, and when to change the subject. At its heart, improv is playful, but as you know, sometimes life doesn't play nice. Your reaction to a "worst-case scenario" elicits an uncensored response from your fellow improv partner. And so, we must be on our toes—ready to react to this emotional volley.

After fifteen years, I know this: Marriage partners act as both muses and mirrors for one another. Cindy inspires me to write a new blog entry for writeonfighton.org every week. She also reflects my fears and vulnerabilities. Seven years ago, a bubbly thespian from New York City walked into the room and presented us with an unfunny scene to act our way through. We were a married couple, had three kids, and one of us was just diagnosed with a rare, progressive brain disease. We looked at each other and took a deep breath.

"Action!"

I cleared my throat and toed the ground, "So this diagnosis sucks."

Cindy replied, "It certainly does."

"I don't know what I'm going to do about it."

"I'll tell you. We're going to make the absolute best of it."

"I think I'll start a blog."

"Life favors the brave."

And the scene went on. Months later, I heard Cindy talking to a friend about my then recent health troubles. She told her "we" had a flare-up. For a moment, I thought she had misspoken, said, "we" instead of "he." But then Cindy explained my recent health troubles to her friend and clarified that the "we" was me.

It now occurs to me that Cindy has been dealing with my health troubles as much as I have. We are still in that same improv scene from seven years ago. When we're sick, we often think we suffer in isolation, in the solitary confinement of a monologue. We get selfish, fall into ourselves, and lash out at anyone who claims to understand.

But this is untrue. I don't suffer. We suffer.

In the vacuum of my troubles, I often fail to recognize that life stretches well beyond my knowledge. Well beyond my body. That my life, our story, is a cornerstone chapter of someone else's story. And we get through it together, scene by scene.

HOW TO SAVE A MARRIAGE

It was romantic as hell. We were finally alone on the beach house front porch. The sun was descending and the sky made grand commitments to the pinks and oranges that stroke only the finest of summer evenings. Cindy sat across from me. I took her hand. The kids were somewhere inside, doing God knows what. It was quiet, and we could hear the distant break of the Atlantic Ocean along the soft New Jersey sands.

I admitted I don't say "I love you" enough. I told her she deserves to hear it more. Eight years of marriage and three children later, I promised that I would tell her I love her every day for the rest of our lives. We held each other's gaze long enough to vaguely remember what life was like before children until one of them threw open the screen door and complained about something a sibling was doing inside.

We both said we would be right there and the child waited, then stomped, turned, and disappeared. This was our vacation. Our moment. The rolling sea. The tender sky. There was no need to rush. It was a scene that unfurled on the silver screen of our imaginations when we were sixteen years old and first began to conjure up a life together.

Like any new resolution, I was all in—with energy and verve and boyish enthusiasm. I planned out how I would slip it casually into a conversation or let her believe I had forgotten about my promise only to surprise her with an "I love you" as she was falling asleep. And for a few weeks, I was true to my promise. But, at some point, I missed a day. Not that I didn't love my wife anymore. I just failed to think of someone other than myself. And, as promises go, failing to keep them one day made it easier to forget about them the next. Until today. My wife confronts, me half joking, half serious, "Why did you stop saying, I love you? Do you not love me anymore?"

I stutter and stumble. I say I'm sorry and promise from here on out I'll say, "I love you" every day for the rest of our lives. And so, I do. For a few more days. But then—, as promises go...

My parents are cruising into their fortieth year of marriage. I say cruising because they make marriage look effortless, like a joyride.

A Sunday afternoon cruise with the top down and the radio up. They tell me the key to their marriage is a little ritual they've engaged in every evening when one of them returns home from work. After a long day, when they're finally reunited, no matter the condition of the household, no matter the company sitting at the kitchen table—the first thing they do is kiss. It's a moment to recognize one another. A moment that is just theirs. A moment to honor their relationship. It's such an amazing moment, especially considering the anarchy of weekday nights when the kids squeal about the house, when dinner boils over on the stove, the phone is ringing, work is emailing, there's a mouse loose in the pantry, and the bills are strewn across the kitchen table.

Life, and all of its obligations, demands so much attention that sometimes you forget you're married. Days pile onto days. The chores and responsibilities mount. There's only enough time to breathe and react, and the thought of thinking about someone else is simply too much. So marriage makes strangers out of us. Our spouse becomes a coworker, one who we occasionally bump into at the copy machine or the coffee pot. Things get awkward. There's a head nod, then a slight smile before you retreat to your own business. How do we avoid such a fate? Like you're always commuting from one draining job to the next.

My parents proved it starts with simple, sincere acknowledgment. They did it, and continue to do it, with a kiss. They proved that marriage only works when you're willing to connect and invest your attention in the smallest of moments.

I tried saying, "I love you" to my wife every day and failed. Failed to create a daily moment that was just ours. Why? Because it's hard. Because it takes real endurance, real commitment, to honor your marriage every day. Because sometimes I take marriage for granted. When life is not romantic as hell, the health of a marriage hinges on those private moments that you create for one another. It's in those moments when you reconnect, rediscover each other all over again.

Original artwork by Haley Armstrong

THE LOVE STORY THAT ALMOST NEVER HAPPENED

You may not believe this, but I always knew I would marry Cindy. Just one look and I knew: Love at first sight. Soul mates. Kindred spirits. A cosmic connection. Whatever you want to call us, I knew from the first time we saw each other, we were fated to build a life together.

However, there's been a problem swirling in human DNA since the reign of the ancient Greeks when Oedipus challenged fate, lost, and naturally, carved his eyes out. It's an inherited belief that, with a certain mix of age and experience, we're strong enough, smart enough, and tough enough to best powers beyond our control.

During my senior year of college, I read Jack Kerouac's *On the Road* for the first time. His images of freedom unfurled out on the glinting asphalt of the open road and intoxicated me. At the same time, I realized I wanted to be a writer. Drinking beer and listening to Pink

Floyd, I fancied heading west, attending grad school at some big university, rubbing elbows with famous writers, moving to a big city, leasing an overpriced one-bedroom loft, and scoring a job as a sports journalist.

I knew I wanted a writing life, but I thought I wanted a writing life on the road. A life that would offer the excitement my life lacked. I felt confined, trapped by my small private college, my hometown, and everyone in it. Including Cindy.

I thought I wanted more.

I'm not proud of myself. I remember, as I entertained a sports journalism life, how much of an asshole I was to Cindy. How reckless I was with our relationship.

As she sat on her bed in her dorm room, white Christmas lights snaking across the joint of the wall and ceiling, I told her she was holding me back. Young men, like the gods we dress ourselves up to be, often believe we are the sole creators of our success and happiness. So we distance ourselves from others. We forge fantasies. We mask our unhappiness and insecurity with false bravado and empty dreams. We puff out our chests, turn our hats backward, and pretend we're in control of our life and that fate is just a motif found in ancient Greek theater.

I yelled at Cindy.

I told her after graduation I was heading west. I was going to be a sports journalist. I wanted a life on the road, going to games, sleeping in hotels, and writing stories. I invented a life that any twenty-two-year-old man would likely invent for himself—exciting, mobile, and bursting with possibilities.

When I told her to let me go, she sat on the edge of the bed and cried. When I told her it was over, she protested. I grew angry, stormed out of her room, marched down to my dorm room, and got drunk with Pink Floyd.

Now, a few chapters ago, I encouraged you to read *The Alchemist* by Paulo Coelho. Though it's by far the most soul-cleansing book I have ever read, I strongly recommend you read with caution. Early in the novel, the alchemist explains to Santiago, a young shepherd, that all people are born with a Personal Legend. That your Personal Legend is your destiny. It's the person you were born to be.

According to Coelho, children are very much aware of their Personal Legend. Whether it's writing, painting, fixing, building, singing, or rodeo clowning, children know, even if they lack the ability to explain it, that by pursuing their Personal Legend they will reach spiritual enlightenment and earthly happiness.

But we grow up. And not in a good way. We question our Personal Legend. Our passions turn bitter. We adopt shiny, plastic notions of happiness because they are easy to assemble and sell at cocktail parties, but with every sale, we distance ourselves from our Personal Legend and sink into a life we soon despise.

I was reckless with my relationship with Cindy. Too scared to accept my Personal Legend. Too self-absorbed to recognize that Cindy and I share the same Personal Legend. Thankfully, she was not. She was too resolute. Too determined. Too clear-eyed on the mysteries of love.

Sometimes she'll read my work and laugh. Sometimes she'll cry. Sometimes she'll laugh and cry all at once. And sometimes she hugs me and smiles. A smile that reminds me of what I have and what I almost lost.

It's evening and I'm writing this at our kitchen table. The kid's homework, half-filled cups and credit card bills are strewn across the table marked with a splatter of forgotten spaghetti sauce that is beginning to harden. There's nothing exciting about the scene. It's painfully pedestrian. Typically suburban. It's the complete opposite of where I wanted to be when I was twenty-two.

But I'm happy now. I'm home. I'm right where I need to be.

TAKING NOTES: A LOVE STORY

In a world with Nicholas Sparks, it's hard to write something original about love. Love is a well-traveled topic: Love is patient. Love is kind. Love is engraved in your heart and scattered among the stars. Love is in the air. Love is an open door. And, if you find the right station, "love is a battlefield."

Anytime you write about love, you ink a fine line between cliché and Nicholas Sparks. So, in my attempt to avoid such a destiny, I can only offer a secret love story about me and Cindy. So secret that when my wife reads this, she will know it was told for the first time.

I've written about my health issues and personal shame and failures, but writing about love is something I've avoided. For me, writing about love is a little embarrassing. A little too revealing. Besides, how do you write about love in such an authentic yet impenetrable way that it won't be dissected, compared, or judged?

Truth is—I can't.

It's simple emotional physics (which should've been a 90s emo band name). To love is to want. And to want is to have weakness. You can't open yourself to love without subjecting yourself to dissection, comparison, and judgment.

I fell in love with a girl when I was sixteen. The first time I saw her standing in the threshold of the blue doorway to her Biology class, I simply knew, in my complicated teenage heart, I would marry her one day. And ten years later, I did.

Even though that story is absolutely true, you may still be skeptical. I don't blame you. It seems too easy and yet, at the same time, too impossible. Too Nicholas Sparks.

So, I'll tell you another story that's more believable. Yet, in some ways, just as fantastical. Cindy and I were sitting at a large round table, the kind guests sit around at weddings. We were in the back of a Las Vegas hotel ballroom, the kind couples rent for weddings except instead of a DJ, there was a UCLA professor at the far end of the ballroom. He was standing on a stage behind a podium. To his right was a movie screen showing an MRI of a human brain, a brain with a damaged cerebellum. A cerebellum that looked a lot like mine.

The room was filled with people of all ages. Some were in wheelchairs. Some clutched canes and walking sticks. The same haunted glow was in everyone's eyes.

Seven months after that earth-shattering phone call, we were in Las Vegas attending the National Ataxia Foundation's annual conference for patients with neurological diseases. Cindy and I were surrounded by people of all ages with rare neurological diseases: ALS, MS, Huntington's disease, brain tumors. Some people sat with their spouses. Some sat with their parents. Some sat alone.

The UCLA professor was discussing advancements in stem cell research as a way of improving and repairing brain growth. Cindy sat beside me taking notes. Her hand moved in small yet amazing ways. She was writing down what the professor was saying as fast as he was saying it. Her penmanship was Catholic-school perfect. Her notes were well-spaced and organized, and her margins were aligned.

It was a secret moment in my history. One I've never told Cindy about. It was a moment of enormous fear, yet as my eyes traced the ink-curls of her words, I found a small moment of enormous comfort and safety. A moment of goosebumps. A moment when I finally realized I was lucky enough to have found a woman who cared more for me than I could possibly care for myself.

It was a moment that gifted me the eventual courage to roll my shoulders back and write these sentences: "Let my cerebellum soften to oatmeal. Let my brain cells explode. Let my eyes go blind. Because there's a girl with green eyes standing in the blue doorway, and she's not moving. And she never will."

And that is what love becomes. After all the romance and celestial promises of the initial courtship, love becomes a lifetime of small moments that add up to make something enormous. But even that seems Sparksian.

A chronically sick man whose hands were shaking, whose body ached, who was teetering on the edge of self-destruction, sat beside his wife in a Las Vegas ballroom. They were high school sweethearts. They had three children together. But in 2013, things had suddenly become much harder.

And yet she still took notes.

As the professor spoke and the screen that held the damaged brain loomed like a thundercloud over the room, Cindy reached with her free hand across the table to hold my hand, to ease my mind, to feel my pain.

Cindy and me in 1996. Six Flags Great Adventure. Jackson, New Jersey.

BEFORE I TURN OUT THE LIGHTS: LETTER #6

Dear Haley, Chase, and Dylan,

I was not kidding when I told you I hope this book does well financially. I hope Oprah promotes it with her Book Club. I hope it's translated into every earthly language. And I hope the royalties from this book will pay for your grandkid's Ivy League tuition.

However, if Oprah does not share it. If there are no translations into Swahili and Farsi. And if there are no royalties for future generations of Armstrongs, I want you to know I wrote the best book I could for you. When I doggy-paddled in the depths of doubt, you buoyed me. You brought me clarity, perspective, and tremendous joy. Your laughter, your curiosity, your love gave me the courage to write what needed to be written.

Like all kids, you outgrew car seats too quickly. Soon enough you may find yourself the parent driving the car, forced to answer your child's questions about semen and death. When that time arrives, I hope this book helps you understand, whether you're a parent or not, that life is simply about learning from all the sadness and all the love in your lifetime.

Here's the hard truth: if not told, stories die. And in these pages, with my failing brain, I wanted to grant certain stories eternal life. This book is my alchemy.

Whatever you do as adults, do the best you can. The world will always need people who try their best and give without expecting something in return. Be liberal with kindness. Live with conviction. Tell, and then retell, as many sincere, funny, and reflective stories that your time allows. Stories aren't only for our children. They're for us, for the world—they enrich our culture and weave each of us into history. Stories instruct. Stories comfort. Stories heal. Stories help us sleep at night.

As I write the final words of this book, I smile at the image of you possibly becoming parents. Your kids just asked if you could tell them a bedtime story. I chuckle as you shift your weight, thinking, and grunting, "Umm—" in the darkened bedroom, under the slow turn of a ceiling fan's blades. I long for the moment you realize, many years from now, that bedtime stories are for the living, and it's your responsibility to tell the world a good one.

Goodnight.

I love you.

See you in the morning.

BEDTIME STORY PROMPTS

I believe everyone is a natural-born storyteller. And I believe telling our stories is an essential exercise for cultivating a richer, more fulfilling life. Here are some prompts that helped me write *Bedtime Stories for the Living*:

Tell a story about a time you failed to live up to your own expectations.

Tell a story about falling in love for the first time.

Tell a story about a scar.

Tell a story about what you wanted to be when you grew up.

Tell a story about moral courage.

Tell a story about your father's silence.

Tell a story about a curse word.

Tell a story about your childhood neighborhood.

Tell a story about learning the hard way.

Tell a story about fate.

Tell a story about someone who died young.

Tell a story about your mother's voice.

Want more story prompts? Visit writeonfighton.org.

BIBLIOGRAPHY

Coelho, Paulo. *The Alchemist*, Harper Collins, New York, NY, 1993.

Hosseini, Khaled. *The Kite Runner*, Riverhead Books, New York, NY, 2003.

Kinney, Jeff. *Diary of a Wimpy Kid*, Amulet Books, New York, NY, 2007.

O'Brien, Tim. "*The Man I Killed.*" *The Things They Carried*, Houghton Mifflin, New York, NY, 1990, pp. 118–118.

Palahniuk, Chuck. *Consider This: Moments in My Writing Life after Which Everything Was Different*, Grand Central Publishing, New York, NY, 2020.

I hope you enjoyed *Bedtime Stories for the Living*. If you did enjoy this book, please leave a review on the site where you bought the book. Research has proven that book reviews increase book sales. And remember, college for three ain't free. Thanks!

Also, if you want to spend more time with me, subscribe to my weekly post at writeonfighton.org.